Emotional Fragments Left Behind

A
Poetry collection

Written by
Chris Sapp

gathered in the year
2006

This book, like all the others before and after, is dedicated to my wife, family, friends, teachers, and other people in my life that have had a profound impact on me, leaving me with feelings I was able to put into words in the passages.

Library of Congress Control Number: 2007907414
ISBN 9780615166032
Copyright: 2007

Phone Call

Sorry I haven't called yet
Been catching up on all I've neglected
My games, my writing, my computer
And ignoring you in the process
That doesn't make much sense
How can it be fair
That in the process of doing something
I make my list of somethings longer
I wish you were still here
Under the sheets and blankets
So I could hold you tightly
But 200 miles away you wait
For me to get off my ass and call
I hope you're not asleep
Time for the phone to ring

Burning a Holc

My wallet is full
It actually looks bulky
Now comes self-control
One week to hold it
I don't need a DVD recorder
Like I saw at Wal-mart
I don't need more swords
Or other piddly items
I need more saved money
Less credit card bills
Less car payments owed
Less college loan reimbursements
Money and I don't get along
I get rid of it quickly
And if by chance I get manic
It will be gone in a flash
Hide it away
In a drawer where I'll forget
And keep it for emergencies
I cannot yet predict

For A

If I knew then
What I know now
I would try to keep things the same
And not correct each blunder
Although many mistakes I've made
Each led me to the present
And maybe a slight change
Would ruin my newfound bliss
Though I can't predict the future
I can believe in...
The power of love
There are no coincidences
God has a plan for me
Things will work out as they should
And promises can last a lifetime
Knowing all this
My petty regrets miniaturize
Because the most important thing
Is the look in her eyes

Man Holes

I used to think
Drain pipes lead to tunnels
Wondrous underground communities
They must have them somewhere
To force such strange ideas in my head
Or just television
Like Ninja Turtles and IT's monster clown
Planting ideas
I used to think
Friends almost grew on trees
Easy to find and keep forever
Until I was betrayed
In a cycle that made me more careful
Which deserved that title
From the list of users and abusers
That fill my life

I used to think
True love an illusion
Impossible a match made just for me
Complimenting my strengths
Understanding each of my weaknesses
To share my smiles and tears
In a relationship defeating time
But I was wrong

Man's Best Friend

Dogs not for me
How can dogs be so stupid
As to wag tails while barking
Can't they make up their minds
Do they have emotions and souls
Or is it just a long list of tricks
Conditioned to respond a certain way
No smarter than a mouse
Sniffing out cheese in a maze
I prefer cats
No mistaking of intention
Not only do they clean themselves
They are independent
Purr when happy, Hiss when angry
Refuse to learn tricks, unless by their choice
More instinct than conditioning
More natural than humanized
Complete with a unique soul

Road Sign
Who made this sign
Thirteen miles per hour
Why not ten or fifteen
Twelve and a half would be middle
Rounding up perhaps
But to an "unlucky" number
Doesn't seem likely
It's a coincidence

Maybe someone like me
Out for a little fun
Laughing each time
They see their sign

Why?

Sometimes I sit pondering
Why things are as they are
Usually it has nothing to do with me
But I'm often blind to the fact
Maybe I should not try
To find meaning in everything
Analyzing beneath the surface
Missing obvious beauty
Sometimes yes just means yes
And no just means no
Requiring a reason
Just a waste of time

A Desert of Memories

It would be nice
If I could take back what I said
Although I get forgiveness
Nothing is forgotten
Every action one takes
Leaves footprints in a sand
Where the wind never blows
And the tracks become concrete
Luckily most choose not
To dwell in this desert
Of memories and past
But pay it no mind

High on Life

This strange idea
That one can be 'high on life'
It's starting to make sense
But it's difficult to grasp
My highs were usually temporary
And had negative side effects
Being high on life
Is all around wonderful
Smiling from anything
Laughing at yourself
Realizing you can't go back
Moving forward with your head up
Each of us is
An unfinished art work
Never quite complete
Sometimes barely begun

Symbol

I wear a ring
Around my neck
On a chain
As a symbol
The ring for you
And chain my hand
Together interlocking
To form another symbol
The infinity
Much like a circle
A path everyone takes
But not all share

Too many tears

Have you ever cried
Until your tear ducts ran dry
Maybe even hours
And not remembered why
Have you ever kept a secret

Because it was better left untold
But soon realized
You just needed to be bold
Have you ever missed someone
So much while knowing how
To pick up a pen and write a letter
Why not do it now
Have you ever let the phone ring
Assuming you know who's there
Not wanting to hear excuses
Is that really fair

Capable

When your image runs through my head
I realize something about myself
I am capable of things you could not do
And some of them are terrible
I can't help you fix yourself
But I can assist in breaking you
Using powerful words like hate
Is that ever the right thing to do
When I imagine your smell
It sends shivers down my spine
To think how much I rearranged myself
So that you would think I'm fine

Pi

Have you ever wondered
If there's any truth
To so many things
We consider factual
Does staring at the sun
Really make you blind
Or does it cause you to see differently
Maybe even better
Those few that know
Don't want the secret out

Do They conspire to fool us
With myths and lies
Then all of religion
Could be based on the words
One person spoke
After a vision from the sun
But they are just myths
No truth to be found
Don't stare at the sun
You'll go blind!

Past

Interesting how the one thing you can't escape
Tends to show it's face at the strangest times
No matter how you try to make the wrongs right
It is impossible to change the past
Each and every second of your life
Permanently stored at least in your unconscious memory
But usually those not so pleasant thoughts and actions
Involve others who can remind you
Short of having total and absolute amnesia
No one really gets a chance to wipe the slate clean
Honestly I don't think many would wish that on themselves
Trading forgetting the negative with also forgetting the positive
Each of us can be continually molded like clay
Add a bit of water and the change can be phenomenal
Instead of trying to forget, one should just try to learn
The only one who decides your future is yourself

Dad's Birthday

Beneath a weeping willow he sleeps forever
No longer burdened with the pains of life
Possibly looking down at me as I visit
On his birthday with pink roses
Staying not even a minute
I pay my respects and move on
This groundhogs day being the fourth

Birthday he has missed
Each year slowly becomes easier
To visit this place of wandering souls

Complicated

When one is young
Often the deepest complications
Are merely misunderstandings
And lack of maturity
Maybe you were never meant
To stay a part of my life
By chance another opportunity
Arises to make things different
I once met an angel
Not only beautiful inside and out
But completely innocent
Felt she was left corrupted
After many years pass
I recognize her glow
Hesitantly gravitate forward
Offering countless apologies
To my sincere surprise
She has grown more than me
And agrees the past is done
Maybe we can be friends
I never thought I would meet
An angel in the first place
But to get a second chance
The feeling is amazement

Normal

At first glance everything seemed normal
Outside and smoking right on time
But from the moment words erupted
I knew it had happened again
Private time alone was requested
But I had already decided to go inside

Discovering once again the truth
Before she even turned around
My job and my personal mission vary
But he doesn't have to know
These eruptions of emotion must cease
Before all of us just give up
This time she will decide
What punishment is appropriate?
And I will back her up
Regardless of his guilt or remorse
Time for lessons to be learned
Lazy Adults cannot blame others (mothers)
When given so many opportunities
To just do the right thing

Uncomfortable

I sat two pews back
Amazed at the pathetic
Excuse for a congregation
That gathered this night
Everyone introduced themselves
A head count of only twenty
Some gave a long prayer
Including in visitors like myself
Quite a large mistake
This was a business meeting
Not exactly what I had expected
When invited to visit church
I kept my discontent hidden
As I picked on my shoe
All the mud I had gathered
With a pen cap
Ending later than expected
And not a single song
Remembering why I say
Spiritual but not religious

Reunion

In less than two years
Then ten will be up
Time to return to those hallways
And classrooms I left behind
Everyone knew me
Yet I was invisible
Just another pawn
Doing as I was told
So much change has occurred that although I appear
A grown up version of that old person
It's a facade that will vanish once I speak
Perhaps the truth and perhaps a blanket of lies
Would it be nice to keep pretending?
I'm timid, afraid to raise my voice
Or to over-exaggerate the new me
Screaming, Sarcastic, and Blunt
These decisions must be made
So that I can be prepared
For whatever it takes
To be remembered this time

Expectations

I wrote something about someone
That now I barely know
And delivered it by email
The day before the snow
Explanation was included
So as to clarify
My intentions pure and honest
Hoping not to say goodbye
Wanting a new chapter to begin
Where I bookmarked long ago
And a friendship to develop
Not fast but rather slow
Waiting for her reply
The deed now complete
Praying that she enjoys it

As it would be some feat
Following a resolution
Chosen at random for me
To grow some new friendships
And have done it for free

No one in particular

Maybe this time I did it
Going over and above
Not keeping my mouth shut
Losing someone I love
Maybe now it's finished
And I should only think
To myself and say nothing
To that girl in pink
Being instead a mystery
Than sharing every thought
Mistakes I can't take back
Just do as I ought
She would never know
If it remained a mystery
I'd be better off
And she would still be free

Bright

I can always see you
Shining oh so bright
Sometimes I only wonder
If you'll vanish into light
Or worse someday burn out
From being too strong too long
I hope it does not happen
It would feel all wrong
For once to see the tears
You constantly hold inside
Only visible in the dark
Would take away your pride

Although you can be brilliant
All of us are the same
We all feel pleasure and pain
And we all have to except blame

Excuses

To actually make up an excuse to escape
To come back to what was my comfort zone
Before I was spit on and hit in the head
Sometimes I wonder what I am doing
I really had a task to complete
But the store is closed
And it was not urgent
I just had to get up
My patience appearing infinite
Is reaching its boundaries
Every condition I must follow
To never do my real job
If it could possibly be embarrassing
Then just hold back and
Make the world appear to be his playground
Even if it isn't

Thanks

I would like to say thanks
But it doesn't add up
Unless one plus one is five
Or I'm in another reality
Putting up with something
And having patience to relax
Help the best way I can
And then move on
That is my job
It is not his
To create situations
For me to fix
Yet I want to thank him

Because he brings out the part
Of me that is expressive
And wants to write a poem
The part of me with feelings
That usually stays hidden
The part of me that cares
About anything

Today's High School

Is this really a high school
Seems only days since I attended
And now here in another fashion
Not as a student but an adult
The intercom begins a message
That would seem imaginary
Students skipping school, no
But just to remain safe, yes!
That was the gist of it
Tomorrow is school safety day
Everyone must do their part
By being totally accepting
No culture or group identified
Just an idea implanted
That the plan wasn't to be tolerable
Seems more like a war zone
Maybe the punishment
Needs to fit the crime
When a group of bullies
Can have this much influence

Stupid

A title can be so descriptive
In this case it's describing the writer
To actually believe his little pep talk
Can have the intended and desired effect
Every time I can't make up my mind
If what he says can be taken seriously

And by the time I do
I am always wrong, AGAIN!
Do I need to lower my expectations
To a more reasonable level
Belittling his desire to reform
And my ability to help that change occur
Should I just continue to do all that I can
Realizing the result will likely be the same
But also that I am no Jesus
And I cannot perform miracles
It has to be
All the parts of him that were in me
That beckon me to continue
This quest for punishment and absolution

Suicidal Thoughts

Please don't make
That kind of empty promise
Making me choose between
My obligation and my opinion
How can I ever be sure
If you're serious
I was sure you would not punch
But you did
My inner clockwork
Must be broken
If I can't tell a lie
From the truth
You can't choose death
It must take you
Suicide is for cowards
Too afraid to live

Teacher

Really a teacher
Or just an imposter
Is this the right field
Or just another job

Questions sprint
Through my mind
About ability
And quality
Being so rude
Letting others laugh
Almost encouraging
The reason they hated school to being with
The reason they are here
Probably the inability
Of some teacher
To control the students

Untitled

What other way of life
Would let me pay attention
But not actually interact
As my pen marks the paper
People around me
Unable to read even this
And then to understand
That would be another hurdle
Am I too complex
Do I need to become
Mentally younger to relate
When immediate gratification
Seems to be the only way
I can break through
The monotony and lack of balance
Between myself and them

Another School Room

Does anyone know what's going on
Or is this just a room full
Of zombies that sit waiting
For the next instruction
While all the capable

Talk to one another
Ignoring their duties
And having social hour
Sometimes I think
People are here to chat
Not for a math class
Or to learn anything
The chatter continues
As I sit quietly
To write and observe
The nonsense

Smelly

Something about that smell
Lingering in the kitchen
Unsettles my stomach
Preparing a gag reflex
Not even able to think
I rush to another room
Sit down and begin
To make myself hungry
Usually it doesn't work
I just force the food
Into my mouth
One bite at a time
Wishing I had a way
To remove that putrid odor
Maybe I've discovered
America's new diet
Transform the scent
From the trash can
Into a liquid
To use as a plug-in

Angry

When I refer to myself as mad or angry
It is not likely anyone would understand

Not because those emotions are complicated
But because of the way I define them
I consider them to be polar opposites of happy
As in complete and total uncontrollable chaos
Worse than what most could imagine me like
And sadly, it's only the tip of the iceberg
Sometimes I feel such utter hate and disgust
That I am afraid to write it down
Not only afraid that I might be "crazy"
Afraid I could be used as a weapon of destruction
When overtaken by this powerful madness
Do whatever is necessary to stay away
Every one and thing will be a target
Until I over-medicate myself to sleep
To pretend like it never happened
And go on with my fake existence

Thinking

Sometimes I wonder what Eric is thinking
But mostly I wonder how he is thinking
Why he chooses to say and do as he does
And what is the real impact I am having
Am I truly ready for role modeling
Will my seemingly endless patience run out?
Do I know what it's like to be in his shoes?
And does it matter in the scope of my job
He's made me laugh, he's made me cry
Each day hello, each night goodbye
Only male who says I love you
Only one I say it back to
He follows rules to make me smile
Tell him I'm proud and walk a mile
Although he can manipulate
It's not his most prevalent trait
Each day at work I get to laugh and have fun
Although he keeps me on the tips of my toes
I could not be happier with another
Especially when he says I'm like his brother

Ticks

As time ticks near
It seems as though
That door I entered
Was to another world
A gigantic empty room
That will slowly fill
With angry faces
And broken promises
With excuses
And lies
With forgiveness
And punishment
With justice
If I believed in it

Where are they

Am I in the right place?
Ten till nine and no one
I feel like a goldfish
Forgetting all every two seconds
Maybe this is a test
Someone appears to me
And they begin to slowly shuffle in
Like robots to a funeral
Not understanding death
They just don't care
Not having emotions
They appear flat
In five minutes it will begin
And with only 3 people
Maybe it will end
Quick and Painless
I don't want to see her
Glaring back at me
Maybe I will just face forward
From the front row

Though I doubt my fear is hidden
It seems to radiate.

On the dot

Nine on the dot
Less than ten people
Seems like a dream
And I want to awake
Time soon to listen
To all the instructions
That I always hear
When in court
Cut off your phones
Do not talk
Do not leave
Do not react
Just sit silently
And wait your turn
To have the law
Handed to you
On a silver platter
Dig in!

Reserved Seat

In my usual seat
Front and left-first row
It seems to be my spot
And being first I took it
Now 10 past nine and the DA is here
Along with the belief
And maybe twenty total people
Defendants, Witnesses, Accusers
They all look the same
Dress up or down
Black or white
Innocent or Guilty
Just a group
I might later get to know

If we all have bad luck
And end up locked up

So much for that

So much for not seeing her
And ten rows back
Right behind me
Staring through me perhaps
When I answer attendance
With deferred prosecution
I bet the anger in her boiled
Not long until I will know
My name's been called
And my motion denied
A continuance to gather evidence
Can this get worse?
Finally done with the large room
I visit my attorney
Who assures me?
The worst is yet to come
I say a silent prayer
Just this once forgive me
While thinking about jail
And hoping for mediation

Untitled

Had I been able to see the future?
I could have gotten so much more
Done in a timely manner
And not been in the mad Monday rush
Each piece of my schedule ordered
So that they form a full day of activity
And one thing missing
Throws a wrench into the equation
It would be nice to be spontaneous
But I have never been that way
Somehow I don't think it would work
I enjoy a sense of control

Which not only comes from a plan
But every person and thing in the plan
Going exactly as it is supposed to
Maybe I am a perfectionist
Not that I want things to be perfect
But I want them to be orderly
One logical step to follow another
In this totally illogical adventure called life

Questions

Is she really the one...?
Is there such a thing...?
Are we both just broken in...?
And comfortable the way things are?
I've never felt quite this way...
But no feeling is ever the same...
Different combinations equal different outcomes...
I know I've been wrong plenty
That is the one thing I am most sure of
I have and will always continue to make mistakes
Nothing is cut and dry and life is almost impossible
Being good or bad overall is very subjective
I will have to make a choice
Whether it be right or wrong
And my choice is her
Till death do us part
Through good times and bad
Through sickness and in health
I want this to last beyond forever
She makes me yearn to better myself

An Old Friend

The longest relationship every maintained
With a female I once thought of
As my best friend and possibly soul mate
Still continues as if uninterrupted
Conversations could go on for hours

Once a record we tried to set
How long we could stay on the phone
Just talking to one another
Our backgrounds different yet similar
And time apart I long to forget
All the mistakes and silly games
I participated in without guidance
Now more than ever before
I realize she knows the real me
With her there are no secrets
And I believe there never will be
The hour we just spent talking
Reminded me how therapeutic a friend can be
How hearing a voice can calm me
And fill me up with life

Long Ago

Back in high school
Sometimes I would sit and wonder
Why does she get all the love in the world
Including all that I had to give
Now I really think
She had almost no one
Lots of so-called friends that felt sorry for her
And many men that took advantage
We never became that close
As I was only a free ride
A way out of troubled waters
Someone under her spell
I don't think my overall effect
Really meant much in her eyes
But to me she was a goddess
Until I decided to walk away
Occasionally I see her picture
And wonder if all that time was wasted
Trying to fill someone up
Who was obviously hollow

Phone rings in the night
Waking me from a needed sleep
My parents enter with upset looks
And give me the telephone, It's her again
Only when she needs something
Although I doubt I can help
Curiosity encouraged me to ask
What is it this time?
She's in the woods close to home
Bleeding and hiding from police
Having slit her wrists she doesn't want to be caught
But I don't want another lost soul
To somehow get blamed on me
So I open my mouth and speak
Explaining to her she has lots to live for
Although if asked what, I would have no clue
Imagining I'm a doctor
Encouraging her to call out for help
And she is discovered and says goodbye
After a brief thanks
Now to tell my parents
"Why do you be-friend these losers"
I try to fall back asleep
But images of her bounce through my head
Life becomes ordinary once again
Until she is released from care
And the phone rings again
She remembered what I did and wants to return the favor
But I am not suicidal
And she can only cause trouble
The variable, I fail to understand
How something so simple
Becomes a complicated mess
By adding only one change, is it so unpredictable
This tiny factor in a huge equation
That infinite possibilities emerge
As it is introduced
The only possible answer
Is to remove the rebel

The unknown
From what has become chaos

February 13th

One month to the day
Until things go my way
At work I'm sure I'll be
Yes feelings oh so free
Twelve days before
I'll have completed my chore
Standing before the judge
And hoping he will budge
Praying for a miracle
To make things hysterical
Like total lack of evidence
Washing away their confidence
Today I found there's still a chance
To be deferred, how I would dance
Leaping, Gliding though the air
Having these thoughts, should I dare
Either way be over and done
In one month I can have fun
Whether free or jailed, supervised or not
Penguin will still continue to rot

V-day

Today is Valentines Day
When I should be dreaming of love
And having a majority of my mind
Focused on my fiancée but it isn't
Instead I'm thinking about my family
But it's still unusual
That compassion and my sister
Are in the same thought
Today I feel for her
Much like myself three years ago
Her engagement is off

And she's taking time off work
A medical leave of absence
To get some needed counseling
And try to make some sense
Of her strange current medications
Those stupid pills
Taken as ordered
That makes things worse
And make depression visible
All she has done for weeks is sleep
I have barely seen her
Maybe she needs some flowers
To know that someone cares

S

The most frequent memory of you
Was the refusal of a kiss
And my angry arm hurling a drink
Slamming the center of the movie screen
That night I drove too fast
Scaring all my passengers
Actually being stopped by a resident
That proceeded to cuss me out
Driving in mindless circles
Re-thinking the events of late
I lost the discontent man
And found my way home
Almost every meeting from that day
Involved the part of me I want to forget
The drugs and immature behaviors
That are no longer a part of me
I struggle with the decision
Should I forgive and forget
As so many have done for me
And give you another chance
Or are you only a second thought
Likely to never be a true friend
What I saw in you then were just problems
And now I know you can't be fixed

Three years

Three years have passed
Since that woman I adored
Became the one that I abhor
Now maybe this holiday I can renew
Three instances she cheated
Maybe trying to give me a hint
That thought I was hers she was not mine
This year I smile not having to argue
Three tears I'm sure I shed
At that point on all the coke
Willing to try anything I could smoke
To put her out of my mind
Three times they say a charm
I push away her last memory
And open my eyes wide to see
All that is in front of me

Curious

Did he follow through
Finding her a present
From stuff lying around
Somewhere inside the house
I offered Wal-mart
A cute little teddy
Or box of chocolates
Never steered Forrest wrong
But the choice was made
Not to "waste" money
How a gift would be a waste
That I don't know
And back to the question
Did all her dreams come true
Does she really exist
Or knows she's his girlfriend

Nine

You're only nine years old?
But your six feet!
Your nails are so long
And your permanent teeth are in
All those wrinkles
And that huge bag of skin
You proudly shake about
When you feel intimidated
Not to mention your color
As you bask in the light
The browns, greens, and whites
Mix into a strange pattern
Perhaps most human like
Are those big black eyes
Following me like a hunter
What? You're a vegetarian!
Like a modern day dinosaur
But easily maintained
And practically harmless
Little Larry the iguana

Depressed

Being in control isn't always good
You begin to take things for granted
Everything is going your way, nothing could possibly go wrong
And when it does your back where you started
Almost 10 years ago
Suicidal and on the brink on self-destruction
Images of death blinking through your head
Trying to remember why you were happy
What reasons are left for you to live?
Medicine seems more like a way to help
In killing yourself than to bring you back
And every option seems to be the wrong choice
How did I ever fall into this illusion of control?
I just want to wake up and feel good
But this time it isn't going to happen

There are no miracles or magic at play here
This isn't even as simple as karma
It's just the way life is and always will be
And you still can't deal with it
Once again the shroud blinding you from truth
Has been ripped apart
You have to start building another wall
From brick one
And the idea of moving to grab a brick
Is actually scary
My rocks for good luck don't seem to be helping today
But maybe they are
I'm writing and not bleeding
Or getting my stomach pumped
Why can't these small problems have small endings?
Why do I have to keep on when I want to just stop
It will get better
Just remember that and walk away
Within ten minutes you'll be laughing
That this was even written
And hopefully you will delete it
Before you get locked up
Where you could never end it

Hurt

Your like a perfect angel
Radiant and flowing with color
Bringing tears of joy forth
But I am blind
Your scent is that of a warm spring evening
Full of life and fresh flowers
Enough to make a nose happy
But my sense of smell is gone
Your touch is like blowing wind
Softly caressing the surface of my skin
Telling my brain to smile and laugh
But my lips are stitched shut

The hell of enduring you
In my present state
Is worse than any torture
But I am paralyzed
Soul left here gaping
Through this empty shell
That you used to love
That used to be enough

Stray

Approaching like a stray
Starved for nourishment
And full of fear
I help you

Slowly a beginning
Receiving your help
You come around
Tell Secrets

Share with one another
A friendship that will grow
But empty lies
Cause deceit

Approached about the truth
You brandish sharp claws
Try to slash me
Run away

At first a few tears fall
But soon over it
Repeat cycle
Feeling used

Sleep

Like a cancer
Eating me from the inside
Terminal Condition
But I'll smile

Like I'm drowning
In an ocean
Without help or land
But I'll smile

Like I'm trapped
In electrified barbwire
Sizzling my flesh
But I'll smile

Even crucified
Unbearable pain
Without rebirth
I'll still smile

No matter how
You try to hurt
I'll keep smiling
To anger you

Plastic Surgery
Could not even change
This permanent smile
To anger you

Leezard

Everywhere I look
Lizards
At this school
In my mind
And in the trash
Where I left him

My precious pet
A lifeless piece
Of soft cold flesh
Explains a familiar title
The Absolute Uncontrollable

Love Yourself

Do you really have to love yourself
In order to truly love someone else
Or is it just myth without proof
A story kids are told to improve self-worth
But then being in love is different
Loving strengths with weaknesses
So complete and willing
To make the ultimate sacrifice
Must one love themselves for this?
Sacrificing something one considers useless
Is not really giving anything up
It's like a mime reaching the end of a rope
True love involves more than emotions
Yet also so much more than physical contact
It means you realize how much you have to offer
And you choose to give it unconditionally to another

A Prayer

I prayed last night
Twas the first time in months
Maybe longer
I did not expect a thing
Today I was neither
Surprised or disappointed
I know someone heard it
Even if it was just me
Only the answer was not yes

Untitled

How similar the web is to being published
So quick to find and access the information
Not only are some things better left unsaid
Sometimes they would be better if I was dead
I by no means tried to make my pages private
Even advertise to get some more attention
Thinking now about what I should public make
And how much of this blogging was a mistake
As I learn that myself is my only domain
I will begin to take things down and rearrange
Now facing charges for sharing opinion
I need to stay out of other's dominion

Brain Dead

My head might really be empty
Not sure yet if I like it or not
Refusing to focus on the past
But unable to see the present
I sat for an hour just waiting
For some ideas to take sprout
But the silence began to burn
When am I going to learn
Television blends into white
Noise creating a background
Unable to clarify anything
Waiting for a message
Something, Anything
Just a single letter
But my refusal to see the past
Blocks out all senses
Leaving me staring
At a bright screen
Typing in words
Trying to forget
Powerful emotions drive
But can't reach the brakes

Give me a pill for my head
Because I feel so brain dead

A Present

Being anchored by a constant
Something that will never change
Something to stake a life on
The way I feel looking into your eyes

At times anger overcomes me
Pain unwilling to subside
Pain building, forming a wall
Easily broken when I hear your voice

Tears fall like rain in a downpour
Sadness that I cannot hide
Sadness that could make me fall
Your touch like a breeze, blowing it away

Lost pieces of my heart now found
Dusting off each small fragment
Putting me back together
Stronger with you now because I am whole

Stones

In my attempt
To kill two birds with one stone
Used too much force
Each quickly flying away
Gathering friends
And returning to find me
So unprepared
For the impending attack
Now surrounded
Wish the stone could be un-thrown
But it can not
And I stand here defenseless

Their beaks so sharp
As I'm pummeled by their pecks
Talons tearing
Leaving me deformed, alone
Never again try
To kill two birds with one stone
Not even one
Leave things to be as they are

Bested

Struggling to figure out a move
What is it I feel I must prove
Thinking hard and long each step
Beat in five moves while he slept
Gone from the table in a rush
First telling me I'm a blind lush
No goodbye, good game or such
Left me crushed without a touch
My ego does a dumpster dive
How the hell did I ever thrive
On this game of plan and skill
Practice hard I must, I will
Maybe someday in the future
He'll find me so cocky and sure
And these months of practice may
Lead to victory some way

Tree Branch

Scratching the window
Haunted tree branches
Creating Shadows
And causing nightmares
In pitch black darkness
No stars are shining
Just elusive sounds
And absence of light

Clouds

While I simply watch you
I see nothing else
Encompassing my mind
Feeling so full, so complete
Just wondering how great
That which created you must be

Beginner's Lounge

Make one mistake
And it's over
No one playing for fun
Just for points
Everyone striving
To be the best
When the simple truth is
One can never be
Always someone capable
Of simple check-mate
Why I bother
With "beginners"
Who've been playing years
Don't understand mistakes
Even mistakes with my mouse...
Discouraging to know
The brain cells I have lost
Must have been related to chess
And not something else
I could have done without

Untitled

Visiting sights left and right
Seems someone turned off the light
Erased my presence from their page
Trying to get me in a rage
I'm still smiling in and out

Wont hear from me one single pout
I'll just comment in my head
And visit, visit till I'm dead

Remote

Having a remote on life would be nice
Or better, a remote while I was on pause
Like a bystander watching everything else happen
I guess an 'out of body' experience

After a few min of rewind on my life's tape
I am sure I could find a few things to change
Not that I have regrets that often
But I can totally be an asshole

Even if I couldn't actually go back
And just had to sit the sidelines and watch
It would be good for an occasional memory jog
Sometimes they seem to fade in and out

Fast forward could be nice too
But I wouldn't wanna do it while playing
That would show me the total future and erase surprises
Have to hit stop first

And I don't want that to happen
Stopping life would be silly
If it's interesting enough to live it
There is no way I could stop the tape

I guess I already have the best feature
Without a remote or out of body experience
The little red Record Button
The whole reason life is a VCR and not a VCP

Bodyguard

I could be your bodyguard

And always watch your back
I could be your fireman
And douse out all the blaze
I could be your scapegoat
And pick up all the slack
I could be your pilot
And guide you through the haze
But why should I ever try
When we will just say goodbye
Turn around and walk away
Alone with nothing else to say

Sick

No kisses in three days
Someone too contagious
Coming up with new ways
This is so outrageous
Wish we both were well
No strep throat around
Take me from this hell
From which I feel bound

Deaf

Listen to the words
Not the volume of my voice
I'm no fucking stereo
You have no remote
Maybe a message
Of great importance awaits
But you just keep complaining
Please don't yell at me
By the time I'm calm
The window of time has passed
Nothing really matters now
Wish you could hear me

GO

Just run away
Don't even pack
Get lost

Escape from me
Don't look back
Hitchhike

Keep on going
Leave this place
For good

Never be found
No suitcase
Later

For K

Try to out-do me and fail again
Plans just never work out the right way
Maybe in a month, or more, or less
Back where you started, it's such a mess

Wanting to tell you I told you so
Instead I bite my chapped lips and wait
For your explanations and new dreams
Without letting on I know they'll end in screams

Aunt S

Miss Betty Lou
Also known as Sue
She alone can make me smile

In family
Soon married to me
Wish she could stay for a while

Sister has she
Similar to me
Crazy howling at the moon

So young at heart
Makes me want to start
To learn her secrets and soon

From meeting day
Continues this way
So giving and full of life

Hope she can view
Joining of us two
The day Anne becomes my wife

Paranoid

Please don't look at me
Your piercing eyes sting
Remind me of razors
I used to cut myself
Those times so far in my past
Seem like someone else's life
I remember with your cold stare
What I've tried so hard to forget

Bruised

Ocean's waves so rough
Bruises slowly appear
Swollen red pigment
Rises to the surface
Always present but hidden
Underneath layers of skin sheath
Until the constant pressure
This water of pleasure and pain

Vision

Look through this leather (skin)
To the soul inside
So much in common
Failing to see it
Almost like an android
Logic without feeling
Such a Pinocchio
Just longing to be real

Singing to You

Never have I sang a song
Purposely for someone else
But in the span of one day
It has happened thrice

Each time my friend smiled or laughed
Exactly what I expect
It's worth it to make their day
How did they entice?

Just asking is all it took
When did I become so brave
My song always a taboo
Is it really nice?

My voice not hard on the ears
But also not a diva
Karaoke maybe now
What is your advice?

No End to Tears

Her tears never seem to stop
A pain I can't imagine
Should I run or help, be still or pray

I just do not know

Lost that I know not the words
Too slow to ever escape
Does God really listen to me?
Am I just a fake?

Silence creates only itself
So it can't be the right choice
But from the corner I'm backed into
I may have no voice

I do believe time can deal
But one can never forget
How much time they spent trying
To get over it

A Long Time

It's been a long time
Since our paths last crossed
Years with just a thought

Running into you
Memories rush back
Remind me of a past life

Treated with respect
More than I gave you
And I thought I was caught

Reassuring smile
After a brief read
Tell me you don't have a knife

No ill will toward me
Just want to catch up
Today it felt good to be wrong

Picture Girl

I know her only by her work
Her eye for each beautiful place
Visit as often as I can
To put yet more smiles on my face

This female and her camera
Catching each scene with the right light
Showing what life is all about
Be it morning, noon, or night

She reads my poems somewhat often
Such wonderful things will she say
One more person I call a friend
In hopes that it might make her day

Please don't ever give up on art
The world's loss would be such a shame
If you find nothing to capture
Remember that I know your name (well your first name-lol)

Honesty, Always Best?

While it would be nice to make everyone happy
Sometimes that just cannot be
Try telling the truth rather than being sappy
And things work out best you see

Just being polite can only take one so far
Choose instead the brutal truth
It can be worse than death or as bright as a star
Without ending up a sleuth

Don't draw conclusions, without each and every fact
One side is never enough
Learning how to handle your problems with tact
Can easily become rough

Misunderstandings can be for a lifetime

Forgiveness never achieve
Sticking to honesty is the way I rhyme
And truth is what I believe

Backup

When someone needs help they will ask
Until then just empathize
Venture not out into this task
You will not win any prize

Backup is only empty words
Drama is all it can make
This foolishness is for the birds
And I've had all I can take

Why should I be afraid of you
Your not exactly close by
What you think is not even true
And I don't care for your lie

Getting involved when not in need
Just another waste of time
Stop thinking of your own greed
And making the others mime

It could have just ended quickly
Until you joined the parade
Now we're all left feeling sickly
What a stupid masquerade

Another Place

The blogosphere is another universe
In that statement I must agree
It however is not just a wonderland
Unless one is too blind to see

Post only for yourself if you want to find

The wonders of clearing one's mind
In that a blog is basically a journal
So that others will find it dull

Not attention is gained by posting real life
Only when one attacks issues
But then can come chances of unwelcomed strife
That leaves you crying with tissues

Being online you are taking a big chance
So be sure you're ready to dance
Not paying attention for just a moment
Could invite others to your tent

Always be sure that you hide all of your tracks
Who knows, there may be some dangers
In sharing your most intimate thoughts online
To be read by many strangers

It happens Again

Why do I have to make so many mistakes
Why do I assume instead of think
If you really knew what I have done
You would think I've had a drink
I lost another friend today
Or what I thought to be a friend
Now I see that the slightest mistake
Can bring that to an end
I sit here crying wondering why
This always happens to me
I try too hard to be perfect
But shit is all I see
A lesson I should have long ago learned
Has to be forced into my head
It matters not what others think
God will hold me when I'm dead
Too much time wasted to impress
Those that should not matter much
I feel as though I'm a clumsy giant

Breaking everything I touch
Today I promise not to assume
Not to take these chances more
Curiosity once killed the cat
I must learn how to ignore
So if you catch me drifting
Or just not seeming that I'm here
Just know that I am listening
But afraid to respond from fear

Ripple

When someone holds back the truth
It is, in reality, a lie
And a small crack begins
Like a pebble striking a pond
Initially the splash is minimal
But the ripple continues outward
What is called the butterfly effect
And it's unknown influence can be enormous
With more lies comes more cracks
But even one can be enough
A chain reaction beginning
When heat or frost causes it to swell
This slow expansion widens
Although not yet broken, it is imperfect
It has no integrity
A touch could shatter it to pieces
Glass sealant does not work on a person
The false words cannot be taken back
Think of this and tell the truth
Do not give one's self a crack

Untitled

If I believed in reincarnation
And knew what you would be
I would exterminate the species
Even if it were humans

You left me here, jaded and alone
So many questions left unanswered
And hate does not begin to describe
How I feel about you throughout me
From the highest point of a hair on my head
To the lowest point of skin on my foot
This emotion, no words can describe
Fill my body to the core and radiate outward
Sometimes overcome by this power
I wonder if I could change reality
With only a simple thought
Too afraid I hold back, reclusive
Love has no place in the new me
And slowly I lose touch with reality
Then awaken warm in my jacket
But immobile in my white padded room

Puppet

I don't enjoy being your puppet
A toy that is usually ignored
But expected complete devotion
From me to you at all times
These strings are my prison
And all my movement comes from your fingers
Sometimes I would rather not move
And sometimes a voice would be helpful
How overwhelmed you might be
If you understood love and friendship
If you were mature enough to respect me
I know it would be too much at once
causing the walls of your protective shield to crumble
revealing only a confused and spoiled child
Who worried too much about material things
And missed out on social skills class
If I was the puppeteer
Be assured you would miss out on nothing
But blinded by my love for you
I restrain myself in the corner
Until you come again.

Untitled

For once minutes are creeping by
Each seems to last hours
And each hour months
Will this day every be over
The phone rings and it's you
But you are too busy to talk
Just a quick hello
And back to timeless time
Hurling my watch into a corner
I hear some freakish noise
A small being from the shadows
Approaches me slowly
Growing in size and clarity
"It's time to wake up"

Mirror

What happened to you
Everything is backwards
Inside out and twisted
Are you back in wonderland?
Your reflection doesn't mesh with me
And I'm wishing I had never bought you that looking glass
Now that the actions have been taken
Can it be un-done?
This side of you I never saw
Well I hope it begins to understand
How difficult it is to be you
And that no one else is qualified
While your out chasing rabbits
Talking and having tea with caterpillars
I'm left here trying to explain
Why your just staring at a wall laughing
I can't tell them the truth
But then again I'm very unsure

If I can do anything at all
But sit helplessly and watch

Looking Back

When I look back at my 26 years
I stumble to find reasons for my behavior
How six years of my life were wasted
And could, in turn, later shorten my life span
I am of course referring to the "college years"
Which by no means were a total waste
Just the time, energy, and money used on drugs
Those horrible things so far from my new reality
The behavior created a crossroads in my life
Often I had to choose between right and fun
Immediate gratification had it's hold on me
And I've decided, I do regret what I've done
how could my life have been so miserable
That I would turn to drugs to escape
Sometimes binge-in for months without fresh air
Wasting away to almost nothing
So many times I could have died
But nothing deterred me from my quest
Maybe if I escaped long enough
There would be nothing left to come back to
One day I woke up and just quit
No magical solution or help group did it
I met the woman of my dreams and wanted to change
And life no longer seemed like a burden, but like a gift

The Park

Wind whistling so I can't hear voices
Ears probably too frozen anyway
Except for the constant traffic
Speeding by on a neighboring street
The grass appears covered in tarnish
And there are no lights
Thorned vines look like barb wire

This whole place needs a shoeshine
Dead leaves still clinging despite the gusts
There is a training course beside the track
With a concrete pipe that is spray painted
Jesus is a Fraud
The tattered nets in the soccer goals
Could never catch a ball
There are eerie power lines overhead
Complete with a gate as if this park was nice
This entire time observing the scene
My friend chatters about an imaginary place
Where things are bad for everyone
And I realize that means it's fair and equal
Unlike here

Mania

Being highly manic
Is similar to a drug
LSD (acid)
Except instead of thinking too fast to speak (addicts mumble
incoherently)
One speaks too fast to think (talking to hear your own voice)
Rationality is gone
Anger can come from a minor irritation
Extremely open talking is considered normal
Along with a lack of respect
For yourself and everyone else
This state is unhealthy
Although occasionally it's just extreme glee
Usually other factors are at play
And are not noticed
Until it is much too late
Medicating mania is even more tricky
Because most medications create a flat line
A state void of all emotion
Mood stabilizers are very scary
I know this from experience
Although I like being manic usually
The energy, and outgoingness

I realize it's not safe
And that treatment and help are necessary
To appear to be whatever normal is

Change

I wish you would change
But it doesn't seem you can
Maybe if you stopped breathing
The exhalations would cease to be lies
Never have I seen someone travel
So far down a spiral staircase
Into another dimension
Where return is not only unlikely
But maybe impossible
I shutter to think what it's like to be you

Alone

You appear as if you are behind a one-way glass
Oblivious to everything and everyone but yourself
Never have I seen such a complete mystery
But you won't be the first love for me
We exist in different planes
I wonder if we could even hold hands
Now you have my one and only heart
But many before you have had it as well

A Mound

A mound of dirt
Covered with flowers
Pots turned over by wind
Still no marker
Six feet under they say
My dad lies in a box
No tears are coming

As if it has been months
But only eight days
And only six underground
I wonder if he can hear my footsteps
Circling around thinking I re-arrange the flowers
Trying to make some symmetry
This need for order overwhelms me
But dead flowers don't look nice
So I lean against the tree
The one he lies under
And I say goodbye again
As I will be for months

No More Chances

No more chances
Now he's gone
No instruction
To mow the lawn
No more hellos
Or goodbyes
No more truth
And no more lies
No more laughing
At or with him
He is dark now
My lights are dim

Wondering

Right before he went under
John placed a statuette on the casket
A miniature Buddha
Was this some sort of joke?
I remember all the statues and symbols we have
Our strange family, but was this warranted?
Did it offend anyone?
The fact that I noticed it makes me wonder

In a Christian burial would it stay?
Or later be removed and trashed,
or kept By some pastor or gravedigger
Who thought it was a pagan symbol
There are too many questions left unanswered
When someone has to leave unexpectedly
Why this or any other queries exist
Only God may know…But I still wonder

A Dream

Last night I had a dream
I opened the basement door
Where I found him lying, lifeless
But he was sitting on the sofa
It was too much
An immediate rush of confusion
It could not possibly be real
Telling myself NO! I awoke
I can't get these thoughts out
They chase me even when I escape to sleep
Making the repetition ever closer
Is this punishment?
Did I resolve all of my issues?
Or is it just all the conversations
Which only have one subject?
And contain all the same words
I want to forget about it
And occasionally, I am distracted
But all the paths lead back
To the same old painful place

A Boy

There was a boy that had a dad
Just like any other boy
Sometimes happy, sometimes bad
Just like any other boy

Days passed like minutes, years went by
And the boy became a man
Trouble came and they both did try
To solve it as it began
But time too fast without a pause
Left so abruptly one day
So many things without a cause
The man had no words to say
So far this is just a story
And the chance still remains here
For it all to end in glory
Forgetting all the fear
A smile here and a kind word there
Could make all the difference
If they really began to care
Everything could make some sense
There was a boy who had a dad
And the boy became a man
There was no time for thoughts so sad
So he wrote them on this pad

Second Visit

Now there is a marker
With his name and a date
Things are not much darker
Slowly subsiding hate
Grass has started growing
Back where it was before
Maybe it's just knowing
He's there that makes me sore
Stone not in a straight line
Is my biggest complaint
Still from the ground a sign
Now's not the time to faint
Pull yourself together
And just go on with life
He'd be proud you found her
The one to be your wife

Leave me Alone

Don't try to comfort me with words
Your sympathy is for the birds
I hope no person has to deal
All this anguish, it is too real
Specific situation not
Even easy for a robot
To lose one's father is a curse
Finding him all alone much worse
Can you begin to understand
How hard it is to be a man
Hold all those tears down deep inside
Speak words to mother that he died
Try CPR call 911
When they arrive it is no fun
Quietly watch them stare like cats
Caught in headlights, lower their hats
The thing they could do they ignore
Cover the body on the floor!
And the doctor to my dismay
Determine cause of death?, no way!
Call it natural, ignore the fact
That he was lying on his back
Food near by, it would seem he choked
But all they care is that he croaked
No closure in this ruthless game
So turn your backs away in shame
When down my road you take a walk
Come back and see me, we can talk

Untitled Dad Poem

It's been over three years
Since he passed from this Earth
Sometimes I still wonder
If he is still watching
Does he have emotions
He wants to share with me

60

Do I really listen
Would I know if he spoke
Some believe in just death
And rotting in the ground
Others think of heaven
But can he make a sound
Many would point to hell
Because of his choices
More think he's been reborn
And just can't remember
Or his life energy
Has moved to another
I don't know what to think
Afraid I might be wrong
To me what matters more
Is how he lived his life
Although he made mistakes
He was a good father
For me he always tried
Until the day he died

About Blogging

Someone told me
"If you build it they will come"
But I am no Kevin Costner
And this is no Field of Dreams
My patience daily grows thinner
Although abundant at work
Most of my efforts are in vain
I just can't seem to make it happen
I am considering asking others
If I can just join their site
So maybe my ideas will rub-off
Off of me or onto others
Either way, I want to clear my mind
And that is getting accomplished
The question is how much time to invest
Before I actually have an audience

And I just wasting time?
That I could be using
To make my fiancée happy
And improve my chess game
Maybe a vacation is in order
A vacation from the computer
I need to re-discover myself
And stop focusing on the past
For it is dead and encased
In an impenetrable wall
With no doors or windows
No way in or out

Permission

How vengeful I could be...
But maybe she was right
It was an honest mistake
But hindsight is 20/20
Uncomfortable, she moved
Leaving but a bread crumb trail
Before the birds arrived I followed
Was it curiosity or spite?

Every anonymous could be me
Any address can be changed
A whole new persona invented
Just to be an asshole
Not this time
I resolved not to get angry this year
Presently I plan to follow up on it
My plans could always change

She has kept up her end of the bargain
Well, to the best of my knowledge
We still have some shared "friends"
I'll assume our "disagreement" stayed private
So I will keep up my end
And allow this drama to leave my head
Go back to my "old" life

Leaving things just "as is"

I however will never forget
How strange it must be
For someone to know your name
Without permission

Another Place

Find me an island
Without this winter
I don't need cold and snow
A picture would suffice
And in this place
No summer would be nice
All the heat and humidity
I could do without
Just two seasons
Autumn and Spring
Would be plenty
Of what I need
If such a place exists
Then please take me there
Otherwise in my dreams
I will visit it my share

Holding your Breath

How long can you hold your breathe?
I'm up to a little more than a minute
It comes in handy in so many situations
Where there is more to inhale than air
If you find yourself covered in smoke
You will be less damaged
Or if there is a putrid odor
Don't breath until you escape
But my reasons are less literal
Probably too abstract for most
Like when I am surrounded by lies

Don't want any more of those
So I just hold my breath and leave
Same applies for negative energy
Of all shapes and forms
Do you ever hold your breath?
It may seem trivial and silly
How about maybe you give it a try
And once back in a non-charged area
Alone once again you can breathe

Line

The phone rings, I want some gum
I have to use the bathroom
There are so many reasons
To get out of the line
But if you give in
You'll lose your space
Returning afterwards to the back
Almost like last place
Have you really considered
Where the line is headed
Did you carefully examine it
Or just follow the crowd
Maybe you could start a new one
Pick another that is less crowded
Or decide life is more important than a place in line
And you need not follow every sign

Hypnotic

Can you really be hypnotized
Does it mean your mind is weak
Would you remember what you did
Or wake up completely changed
I believe in the power of faith
In it all things can come true
Like the belief that smoking calms your nerves
When in reality, it only fills your lungs with tar

Maybe smokers should re-think things
Try to change their natural response
To something more appropriate
A re-conditioning of sorts
Perhaps a gag reflex or headache
Severe pain in the chest and lungs
You could decide for yourself
If you were willing to believe
In the power of hypnotism
The visit to a doctor may cost much less
Than continuing to support your bad habits
After all, your brain does control your actions
So it really is "all in your head"

No Fence

While on one of my daily walks
I noticed an inconsistency
The small highway's overpass has a fence
Yet the large highway's overpass does not
Did anyone think hard about this
Was there a conscious decision made
That attempting suicide on a big highway
Is more acceptable than a busy road
The cars are moving much faster
The traffic is higher and more constant
The drop off is much further down
But the road's overpass is beside a park
We don't want children to accidentally
Fall off a bridge to die
Ye,s if adults are willing to walk a few blocks
There is no problem
If it has not happened yet
I'm sure it will someday
And the headlines on the news
Will probably still make no difference

Pretend

I for one choose to refuse
To pretend to be someone I'm not
No more convenient lies
Or even half-truths without all the info
I'm just going to be real
Blunt and honest whether necessary or not
It seems to be more hassle free
To be the same at all times
With the exception of Halloween
I don't agree with masks or disguises
An untruth can only last so long
Before it crumbles before the questions
Why Why Why...
And regardless of the answer
It is never good enough

Just for Kicks

Imagine yourself enraged and dangerous for a moment
And that you travel with weapons on hand
Maybe you go into a bar
And some drunk jerk starts something
Do you walk away or warn them
And if they make the first punch
Do you fight back or turn the other cheek
Hoping for it all to end
These hypotheticals often run in my head
When I find myself angry
Just as they did back in high school
Concentrating on the number of ways to take someone out
After I had been embarrassed or insulted
And thought of nothing more than revenge
In that bar one might return to the car
And pick up that handy weapon
Re-enter and demand an eye for an eye
With a gun or knife at your side
But in school you don't have that option
Or do you?

For Mom

To the person I've loved longer
Than anyone else in the world
To the only person I would give up my wish
If there were a genie in the lamp
For the one that raised and nurtured me
To the best of her ability
For the one who is always fair
And when I need her is always there
To the woman who suggests and not insists
Allowing me to learn from my own mistakes
To the woman who worries more for me
Than I could ever worry for myself
For my mom who cooks and cleans
Understanding my slang, knows what I mean
For my mom know that I'll never
Cease to be your son forever

Little Things

It's the little things that keep me going
And make my life seem so worthwhile
The phone calls from friends in need
That can be cheered up in just minutes
But I usually continue to talk with
Because I am getting more from helping
Than they could ever get from me

It's the little things that drive me crazy
All the minor details that sum perfection
Always wanting everything to be fair
Pursuing the quest to be just a little different
When I end up looking and sounding like a clone
Angry that life does not play my game
And that control is just an illusion

A smile can mean so much more
Than even a million dollars
If it's from the right person

At exactly the right time
How I long for the ability to see
Through this coarse reality's two way mirror
And know when those moments are

Keeping the little things at the forefront
Helps to mask the gigantic problems
That surround each and every breath we take
Making this existence seem futile
Thanks to those little things
I might be able to remain so blind
As to not see the forest for the trees

How True?

How true is your love
Would you be willing
To drop whatever you're doing
For just a conversation
Refusing to use excuses
And doing your absolute best
To have a smile on your face
Even if it's only a lie
Sometimes I wonder
What true love is
If all my previous assumptions
Point me in conflicting directions
The inability to stop transference
Of anger from one person to another
Is a skill I have tried to work on
And after years I'm still not finished
How can I expect the one I love
To read my mind and flip a switch
From whatever is going on currently
To a totally unrelated function
Has anyone before her
Or anyone in the world
Ever had a sympathy detector
Or an "I love you" button

Noise

Sometimes noise is soothing
To know you're not alone
That if something should happen
The world has not stopped
Silence can be wonderful
But also full of deceit
Negative energy makes no noise
But can disrupt everything
I enjoy some background noise
Like the filter in a fish tank
I enjoy hearing someone snore
So I know they are breathing
I enjoy the hum of a computer
Telling me the power is still available
I enjoy hearing voices
Even if they're just in my head
Too much noise can be bothersome
But when compared to utter silence
Noise is a small price to pay
To remind me they are alive.

Actors

As Judas did with Christ
Sometime I deny myself
Unable to realize the one truth
Only I can change myself
My refusal to feel self-pity
Only encourages my frustration
If I could I would just cry
But the tears are never there
Often I sit trying to channel
All of my energy and emotion
Into my eyes
Praying for one lonely tear drop
This continuously angers me
Not able to feel enough to produce tears
Yet any movie happy or sad

Turns my pupils into water buckets
Often requiring me to use wasteful amounts
Of tissues wiping dry my face
For something that isn't real
Just a scripted art form
I wish each ordinary person
Had the innate ability
To catch me hook, line, and sinker
As the actors often do

Guilty

I wish I could enjoy these gifts
And not see them as reparations
Some way to pay me back
For what I've done for you
Payback does not factor in
To the relationship we share
I do not want your charity
Nor a silly peace offering
Just the love of a friend
And ears to hear me talk
What you had in the beginning
But lost along the way
I too am guilty
Of trying to buy my way out of trouble
But when we are both broke
How will this continue?

Someone

Repetition seems to keep him going
As he longs for a return to familiar places
And seemingly friendly churchgoers
Always welcome him with open arms
In an attempt perhaps to fit in
He mimics others often repeating phrases
And when anything negative is spoken of
A normal response is "welcome to my club"

Almost like he has explored the whole world
Knows of everything bad that could happen
And even has experienced it from your shoes
When in fact he is quite naive
Very comfortable with any thing constant
Often re-reading the hours of operation
For every space that he could possibly visit
Even making imaginary schedules of his own
He wants to be on time or early
Appreciating those who can help this happen
Minutes alone and bored appear as hours
But when engaged and happy time flies

Magic Bottle

I wish I had a magic bottle
To capture all the tears I've shed
So I could at least convince myself
That crying is still possible
Now only when totally overwhelmed
And so off balance I can't think
Do they dare to appear
Which is better than nothing
Yes still totally unpredictable
And unable to be replicated
Those last few defense mechanisms
Before I actually lose my temper
Do I carry all of my experiences
So heavy constantly on my shoulder
That I am indeed forever changed
And plain immune to being sad
Except to protect me from anger

A month

Tonight marks the last eight days
Of the worst month of my life
Where any answer would be better
Than the time spent waiting and wondering

I guess I should be happy
That I am still able to sleep
My mother can't get any
Often waking at odd hours to watch infomercials
This overwhelming stress I feel
She shares it with me
Yet it does not lighten the burden
Of carrying it around
Instead it intensifies it
Knowing my mistakes effect not only me
But each and every person I am in contact with
And this month may have no quick ending
It could change into more months, or years
Trapping me inside its grasp
Tempting me to show my hidden side
Beckoning me once again to lose my cool
Others pray for me daily
Or at least say that they do
But I have seen no divine intervention
Only signs that the worst is yet to come

Back Then

What happened to those days
When anxiety would conquer me
When fear would fill my body
When I could do nothing but cry
Not only tears but heavy breathing
Running nose and hyperventilation
Those kinds of extreme circumstances
Seem to have left my life
Having stage fright wasn't so bad
It gave me a time for release
To just weep away all the bad
And be left renewed and half empty
Now I would welcome back such feelings
If only for a day
To be able to soak myself
In saline water from my eyes
If only I hadn't wasted it

On book reports and presentations
Piano and guitar recitals gone wrong
Their might be buckets left

Blind

Occasionally I think being blind would be nice
To only have four senses deal with the world
All the angst and hatred of society
Could for once be virtually invisible
Unfortunately I think being blind
Would only allow me to see more clearly
Honing in on my other abilities
Making me almost super-human
That part of my brain
Would surely find a way to assist
The parts that were left
Rather than ceasing to function
Maybe then it would be even more painful
To make it through an ordinary day
Another day completely balanced out
With lots of happiness dulled by lots of pain

Up to you

Life is full of trials and tribulations
More than I care to think about
But to actually lesson their raw number
One would have to stop testing others
Sometimes they are necessary
To know if someone is lying
A slight twist of words
Can be just the trick
Sometimes reverse psychology
As cruel as it can be
Brings real thought to the surface
Instead of automated responses
Still there are days
When I wish you'd just be you

This ever-changing and evolving person
Never really behaves the same way
One day you pass a test the first time
But fail five others you had mastered
And I wonder if I will ever understand
What it is that makes you tick

PHIL

So many things he has obviously done right
Should easily outweigh this one inequity
When thinking logically it appears so
But logic has long been ignored
Meeting and marrying her mother √
Deciding to have children √
Providing for them and raising them √
Pursuing a dream he always had √
This is only a small relevant fraction
Of all his completed positive deeds
And without even one of them
I most likely never could have met her
But…now he chooses to stay at home
So full of a long-ago lost ego
That he can't let go of his past
And move forward into the present
Offers for work are beating down the door
Only none of them are good enough
So he continues to pursue this half-baked idea
That God himself will stand down and let him take over
Why it is everyone but him can easily see
That any job would provide an income
To help out those he loves while continuing to look
For this invisible dream job
Meanwhile she and I wish for miracles
And perhaps push the wedding plans away
To a back burner waiting for that day
When he can once again stop being selfish

Good Teacher

A good teacher I could never be
It would require a lack of hypocrisy
One thing I currently do not possess
Able to teach others the simple rules
That I refuse to follow
Setting an example by one day
And discontinuing it when un-scrupulized
Causing myself pain and disappointment
Becoming one of the assholes
Who can sit it out and can't take shit
Was never my intention
But it has become my outcome
To actually live by the rules I preach
Is exactly what I need to be doing
Yet somehow I become lost from the path
And end up going in circles repeatedly
Sometimes until I get so dizzy I fall
Relax and take a much needed break
Try to pull it all back together, get my bearings
Until the next crossroads
Confused and without a map
I strain to remember what the rules are
And wish the one who had taught me
Was only an arm's length away

Sunset

As the sun sets
The sky erupts with reflections
Light mixing with the filthy air
Creating what may be new colors
The clouds in perfect placement
Form backwards rainbows
How beautiful the heavens are
Helping me ignore this place
I silently sit and peer upwards
Being wrapped in the magnificence of it all
The huge ball of gas and fire

75

Is only a flicker like other stars
Depending where one is sitting
Perhaps in far away galaxies
Our heat source is invisible
Even with a high powered telescope

Hospital

Too much chattering
To hear myself think
Children and adults
Waiting for their turn
Re-reading old poems
Seems to be no help
Do I need the quiet
To think more clearly
Maybe some emotion
Whatever it may be
Could jumpstart my engine
To write some poetry
Instead I just listen
To the bits and pieces
Of gossip and conversations
People share openly

Taking the Stairs

Stairs mean lots of things to me
Mostly just memories of symbolisms
Of people I pushed or kicked down them
And my ongoing journey of climbing
Sometimes I prefer to take the steps
Than be lazy and motion sick
From riding an elevator
Not to mention they seem safer

Waiting room

People afraid of "cooties"
Getting up repeatedly
Moving nearby
Or across the room
To escape the quiet stranger
Minding his own business
Maybe he is waiting
Terrified and alone
Praying for someone
To just say hello
Instead of retreating
Like he is the enemy

Still hope

Just saw one of the few
Remaining truly nice people
Seeing a new window open
But waiting in her place patiently
Until those in line before her noticed
And quickly walked forward
To begin another miserable
Wait for the doctor.

Skeletons in the Closet

Sometimes I like to ponder
The worst surprise possible
One statement with enough power
To completely change everything
Everyone has them
Skeletons in the closet
Painful and harmful memories
That they've wallpapered over
Maybe moving to a new place
Assuming even a new identity
Attempting a fresh new beginning

But second chances never work
They backfire like a mis-loaded gun
Blowing up in your face
Destroying the fresh paint job
And exposing the truth
How many people do I know
That choose to lock away the past
And if I found out
Would it make a difference

Someone 2

Always walking
Usually oblivious
Just listening to tunes
And grinning head forward
A horn honks
Hand goes up
They must know him too
Yet another wave
Maybe imagination
Or need for attention
Causes stories to arise
About the fallen angel
Out for his blood
I'm not so sure
Maybe ignoring him
Yes using public roads
How unfortunate
Maybe 1 in a 100
Of those he encounters
Is not a friend

The 1st Time

All of the firsts
Except for the big one
Came from a game
Truth or Dare

My first kiss
My first unclothed female
My first crush
My first exposure
Although spin the bottle
Could be some fun
And junior high parties
Much more than none
My first surprises
My first positions
My first forbidden deeds
My first obsessions
Always found neighbors
Or friends with sisters
Willing to experiment
During a game of truth or dare

Another Week

I wish I could stay nothing is going right
And although I could, it wouldn't be true
I pretty much still have my one problem
That I brought on myself to begin with
And everyday is beginning to contain arguments
Or at least heated words and lack of patience
Making me totally question my relationship's foundations
And especially my visit out of town this weekend
Seems like it would be more fun to sit at home
And sleep away another perfectly good weekend
This is blinking gigantic road sign reading
Depression in letters large enough a blind man could read it
I really don't see how I am any good today
Not just for myself but for anyone else
I feel like a failure at my job and my relationship
And next week for all I know, I'll be in jail
I can't recall a worse time than now
That's the trouble with writing everything
It helps me to forget the good and bad
When maybe I should be remembering
I hope the tickets have been bought

And my choice is taken out of the equation
If so I'll probably have a great weekend
And I won't be by myself

From a Child

I haven't yet grown up enough
That I see everything as an adult
Sometimes I take a different point of view
And see things a few feet shorter
Where the world is much more innocent
As if I was still a child
These two different views often disagree
Leaving me wondering which is truly the illusion
Being a kid again could be fun
Able to have complete and boundless faith
In any idea without all the facts
No need for reasons or proof
Counting on the giants
To have all the answers
Without the burden
Of knowing anything
Now being one I know they all lie
And my heart is not nearly as open
At what age did I make the trade
Losing my simple ways and following of ideals
To gain the awesome knowledge
That everything must be questioned
And I really have no idea
What is real and what is not

Nervous

Tattered finger nails
But I keep biting
Soon they will be bleeding
Begging me to stop
Knuckles popped so many times
They are aching

Even this writing
Is a small challenge
Leg bouncing up and down
Not wanting to miss a beat
Reminds me of something
Coming down from an upper
And waiting for the next fix
Although it's sadly the truth
I feel like stabbing this pen
Through my empty hand
For thinking about drugs at all
It does not matter how bad I hurt
Nothing can magically make it better
Only postpone the inevitable

Wake up Call

Definitely thinking tonight is a big "Hey!"
It's not nearly as bad as you think
No teeth pulled, no murder, no devil tattoos
I do not have special needs, or a flesh eating disease
Or an amputee or problems with smoking
Maybe you do need to go back to church…
Hearing all of this makes me realize
My prayers are that of a selfish brat
And my problems are mediocre at best
Compared to all these people
That honestly believe in the power of God
And still suffer much more than I

Failed

My plan has failed
I was actually touched
By a religious service
Against my inner will
Just half listening
Was more than enough
To undermine my rules

And change my mind

Someone Else

Thinking he's so smart and cool
Getting involved where he isn't wanted
I agree that he is a wombat
But I would say egotistical, not esoteric
Mind full of dreams that will never work out
Once he enters real life, after college
This self-described BFG will see (Big Fucking Giant)
Maybe he should not have judged me
My misunderstanding of a friendship that never was
And often inability not to take things literally
Even my perhaps breath of privacy
Had nothing at all to do with him
Statements he retracted or deleted
Will not soon be forgotten or forgiven
Though I seriously doubt he and I will ever be in contact
We could not get along, this I know as fact

Eviction

Your silly decision to evict me
To try and hide your tracks
To re-invent yourself somewhere else
A place I would not frequent
In this you have basically succeeded
I found you by accident and left
I purposely stand clear of you and your clan
And I have no clue how things are going
The catch is that I really don't care
Never what you assumed me to be
I have always been uncaring toward you
You are not part of my circle
Much less my inner circle
You're a stranger that talked to me
An acquaintance at best
We shared a few laughs

That was before your imagination
Got the better of you
And before I saw you
As you truly are
The only decision that remains
Is how long I will shudder
And remain prejudiced
When I hear your name

Headache

Popping pills is easy
But it rarely works
To escape this pounding
Happening in my head
Maybe it is sinus
Maybe it is noise
Maybe it is vision
But no one really knows
Reviewing facts I know
Only bores me more
Which brings the ache
Back to the forefront
Need some soothing music
And a walk away
From where I am
This time and place

Strange Numbers

I pulled into the parking lot
Preparing to turn in some paperwork
Happening to glance down at the dashboard
Odometer reading five consecutive six's
Quickly laughing and dictating a note
Into my great new digital recorder
I entered the building and finished
Ready to officially begin my day
No longer remembering my strange sign

Overall yesterday was a good one
A wonderful dinner, a nice walk
More of my new soap opera obsession
And plenty of sleep
I would think that should have been a sign
For Wednesday as bad as it began
But it would be in severe contrast
To the ending I received
Later the irony hit me as I listened to the dictation
Never remembering what I say I held it up to my ear
And pressed play to hear a terrible screeching sound
Followed by the words six, six, six
Coincidence or not

Looking In

What really scares me
Or even has the possibility
Of mentally damaging me
Only myself
Maybe a fear of falling
So I avoid open heights
But in general
I draw a blank
Not being loved
Losing someone I love
People going through situations
Which seem totally unfair
Each of these
Is only my perception
And therefore falls under
That popular category of me
Perhaps a loss of control
The inability to hold back

K

When I observe her behavior
And choose to be objective

I see my own reflection
From years I have outgrown
In just a two week period
She has ended an engagement
Almost moved in with an old flame
Pierced her nose, cut her hair
Under the familiar illusion
That minor appearance changes
Of making the same mistakes again
Could bring her happiness
Although I completely understand
Is it my place to intervene?
If she truly is a reflection of me
My words could never make a difference
Cursed with this inability
To learn any way but the hard way
Someday I pray she realizes
The world cannot be changed
Regardless of infinite will power
The earth and it's inhabitants
All have feelings and opinions
That do not match her own

That Song

Especially the song, but even the band
The sound of her voice and words
Remind me of the one thing you gave me that lasted
The gift I did not return or destroy
Only a duplicate of an early release
That at first made me think only of you
Now reminds me of the moment I shared
Crying in the car with my father
I'll never know if his were tears of joy
Or because the words touched him deeper
But it remains the freshest and most pleasant memory
That I can recall of my father
Although I doubt I would talk to you
If you were the last person on earth
I do not regret all I learned

For our experience together and your gift

Maybe not quite a Miracle

Though I doubt
Something as miraculous
As being re-born again
A faithful Christian
I now again believe
Sometimes things happen for a reason
And if you look hard enough
Your prayers do get answered
One short visit to a church
While working nonetheless
Reopened my eyes
To the wonder I once envisioned
An all knowing and powerful
Energy watching over us
That can help relieve suffering
If you only let it

Days

Wouldn't it be great
If time could pass as it does
On so many soap operas
Seamless and without sleep
Demonic Possessions
Complete mind control
Total memory loss
Being buried alive
One day December
The next February
Did they put the dead child's body
On ice for over a month?
Visits from ghosts
Jobs without even lunch breaks
Coming back from the dead
Dreaming the future

All in one town
Where everyone is related
Making compatible transplants easy
When an emergency arises
The only realism remaining
Vengeful characters caring only for themselves
In this parade of make believe
Where tomorrow is predictable

Really Changed?

I like to think that the *new* me
Is so different from the past
When I looked, dressed, and acted
Just like everyone else did
Slowly I'm realizing that my imagination
Helped me to believe I was ordinary
And although I am now more mature
I'm likely still who I've always been
Have I ever been able to hide anything? NO
Have I always been capable of lies? YES
Have I always gone overboard with gifts for females? YES
Only my shell seems to have changed
I do have much more patience
An increased ability to understand complicated things
My ability to project myself has increased
But isn't that an ordinary part of growing up?
Since second grade it's been obvious when I like a girl
Since high school my patience has slowly developed
Forever I've known lying is wrong but still lied
My comfort level in groups and parties is identical
Maybe there really isn't a new me
Just educated, grown up, and with a direction
The child I started off as
Has begun a life-long evolution

Watching

I love to sit and wonder

What each of them is thinking
While I sit writing continuously
Looking up to make eye contact
How long can I lock my gaze
Before she notices me
And I hear my name mentioned
Through the headphones and music
Now everyone else begins to stare back
I am enjoying this game
Though I have no clue
As to the rules or reasons
I suppose if she is annoyed
Enough to let it show
Then I could be winning
But she has stopped
Oh, no there she was
Looking back and chatting
To all the others
While I sit laughing

Verdict

In less than forty eight hours
This could all be finished
With or without a conviction
Maybe the worry will go back on vacation
But there is always the chance
For another continuance
Stretching this out like taffy
Making each part less sturdy
If that happens I hope a judge
With a familiar face and sarcasm
Will realize this is a waste of time
And that I have more than learned my lesson

A question

There is one question I would pose
To any professional in any field

Do they work for the benefit of others
Or for the benefit of themselves
Is this really a black and white issue
Or is there a tremendous grey area
That eliminates even a chance
For a simple honest answer
One can argue that a doctor or counselor
Social worker, school teacher, or therapist
Is a certain type of person
That just wanted to help others
But really, maybe it's the intense enjoyment
They feel from being able to help
That fuels them to continue
And the patient is just a requirement
One necessary evil needed to experiment
Finding out which strategies and medications work
Creating a reputation which precedes them
Making their life far more simple than before
Perhaps to feel good about themselves
They try be surrounded by those less fortunate
Who need their help to survive
Making them feel better than everyone else
The only career I can imagine
Where one always puts others before themselves
Is to be in some military branch
Where you protect others at your own peril

Contact Lenses

Should I attempt a new record
One that is slightly dangerous
Like seeing how long I can make
Something intended for two weeks last
My contact lenses are for fourteen days
And today is day twenty nine
But I can still see fairly well
Would a new pair make a difference
Blinking back and forth I notice
My right eye is much clearer
Than my left eye

When reading these words
Since the optometrist
Was wrong about the days
Is there a chance
She was wrong about night wearing
Maybe I could leave them in
Just adding eye drops occasionally
Will I go blind
Or is it just another fable?

The old Dream

My old familiar dream
At the time considered a nightmare
Is one of my last lingering memories
Of a blurred line of reality
I would always be walking
Somewhere deep in the woods
Never seeming to know where I'm headed
Or why I am going there
Then I would fall
Down a deep dark hole
Increasing speed for what seemed like hours
Waking up before hitting bottom
But each time my bed was shaking
As if I'd fallen from the ceiling
Could it have been more than a dream
Or just a child learning how
To play tricks on themselves

Workout

Pushing too hard
Will lead to failure
As my exaggerated friend
Discovers on his own
Setting the treadmill
At a speed for a runner
He walks with huge strides

Clumsily trying to keep up
Apparently thinking that
More speed is less time
He asks me how long
He could exercise making suggestions
We have been over this
Twenty minutes is the minimum
Overworking yourself
Was not my idea

No Deal

He looks so composed
Confident and ready
For just about anything
In this scripted game
But in reality not quite
Highly afraid of germs
Maybe the true reason
That his head is shaved
Could this be the cause
For a high rated hit
To be shown in one week stints
Making taking months to pre-record
I miss the curly hair and jokes
The voices from Bobby's World
When he changed from old to new
Did they ask deal or no deal?

Racers

Susan and David both hold back
While racing a length at a time
Slightly unsure who would win
These sprints not real events
Her form is perfect and slow
And his is quick yet sloppy
But they both pace like racers
Reminding me of swim practice

91

Taking a break to rest
Each time they touch the wall
Keeping one another going
A symbiotic relationship

Copycat

Do something
Say something
Give it time
Maybe repeat
Soon enough
The copy cat
Begins to mimic
Whatever it is
Scary to think
How easily influenced
The attention seeker
Can sometimes be
Left wondering
The rhetorical question
Would you jump off a bridge?
If I did it first

Tone

Sometimes the simplest phrases
Can become completely exponentially sweet
When one whispers them softly
Standing close to your ear
Words that might otherwise
Seem totally meaningless
Have a new found value
When barely audible
Therefore the exact opposite
Must also ring true
Similar phrases when screamed
Can be terribly effective
In bringing another down

Even a slight raise in volume
Could be misinterpreted
As hate with intent
Tone is so important
And likely ever more so
When speaking to someone
Than when just writing
Being in control takes practice
And I have not yet mastered
The part of proper speaking
Where words lose or gain meaning

Remember

You don't remember me
But I remember you
Hard to believe our impressions
Of one another could be so different
Maybe you've forgotten what we had
Or just choose not to admit
There was a time we were inseparable
And now my name escapes you
The first time it happened
I pretended like it didn't bother me
But ten calls later still no effort
To simply put my name in your phone
In this world of wild technology
It makes me sad to think
All the memories that we share
Are still not enough
For you to spend the one minute
Entering my name in the phone
Maybe then you could pretend
That you remember me

Aging

Strange when back in halls
Sitting in familiar places

The people walking by
Always appear so young
Maybe even younger than me
Except school is still in session
Are these parents and teachers
Or just family members
Here to pick up the students
That could be the case
But either way I'm seeing
A bit past just the surface
If only skin deep I peered
Then I would not notice
That these strangers appear
As grown up kids, not adults
I wonder when and if
That day will come soon
Where I change from twenty something
To just a straight adult

Something for Nothing

What makes you believe
You can have something for nothing
Have I really been that blind
Only now seeing the truth
If love is not reciprocal
It ceases to be love
And becomes an obsession
You taught me that
How then can you now lie
Trying to get beneath my skin
So you can again reach my heart
It broke for you once already
You're welcome to the remnants
That remain of what we had
But the new me
Is immune to your poison

A true poet

I sat in awe
Head bowed and eyes closed
Listening to a prayer
By an older gentleman
His words flowed
Like a gentle river
Each thought transitioning beautifully
To the next
By memory he covered
Likely all the prayer concerns
And most amazingly
It seemed he didn't even pause to breathe
This man was truly blessed
With the gift of speaking
And uses it only
To glorify God

As you are

If one is truly happy
There is no possibility
For cosmetic surgery
Or wishing for a change in appearance
No thoughts of losing weight
Or of growing hair
No thoughts of enlargements
Or any type of implants
Being truly happy
One would not want
To gather the attention of others
Who did not love them as they were?
Nothing wrong with eating right
Or exercising, proven to help health
But other selfish changes
Can being only jealousy
To those who already care
Those few truly important groups
And they deserve the right
To love you as you are

This Time Through

This time through
They sit in the front
And I take a seat
Five rows back exactly
I would prefer
This to be my final visit
To the familiar place
Where the walls even watch you
Been told by counsel
The full range of possibilities
From almost terrible
To several I can handle
And as bad as I want
To leave headed to work
Staying any amount of time
To end all of the today
Would be well worth it

Prayer

Today I made an honest prayer
Trying hard not to be selfish
Understanding the answer isn't always yes
Yet begging for a way out
I'm sure God heard me
Where ever heaven is
And he has already decided
How to handle my situation
All that remains
Is for me to understand
What his choice was
And how it will be carried out

Face to Face

After a short yet meaningful talk
The guilt over what I have done returns
It has been amplified
Knowing where the penguin came from
For what I have done
Perhaps my worst of all mistakes
I am so honestly sorry
Those words cannot begin to explain
There wonderful people I face
Gave me something to think about
How a father feels losing a child
I believe it will stay with me forever
So cruel, insensitive, and vindictive
Following a path of lies and false memories
I pray this can be a new beginning
And I continue to walk the straight and narrow
I did not get into this field
And pursue careers to help others
In order to find their weaknesses
And exploit them to the world
With assistance from God
I truly hope to one day be forgiven
By all those that I have hurt
And some day make amends

Not quite calm

Although I know they have agreed
To allow me deferred prosecution
I remain unsure if I am eligible
Or if the judge will agree
It is obviously silly to assume
That things will be just peachy
But I must attempt to stay calm
And also to keep breathing
It seems silly to say that
But nervous I sometimes forget
Gasping for air inappropriately

Trying to catch my breath

March Beginnings

Although "it" isn't over
I am beginning to feel relaxed
Like my life can continue
And this might not be the worst day of my life
I plan to make March a true change
Perhaps give up something for lent
Use my community service to help others
And give my life back to God
I hope and pray for the best
I have an appropriate stepping stone
Officially being an adult starting today
And moving forward only with my life

The Judge

Never have I seen a judge so angry
But I feel it was totally appropriate
She saw how giving a plaintiff can be
Considering the awful circumstances I am in
And let them take the situation as is
Deciding if my punishment would be fair
But clearly stating if she was in control
I would be in jail for quite some time
Maybe the community service will help me realize
How horrible desecrating a memorial site is
And how every time they look at it
Part of her memory will be missing

Finished

For getting almost exactly what I asked for
I really don't feel wonderful or relieved
Regardless of walking on egg shells for one year
This reaction is one that could not be predicted

Honestly sorry for what I have done
Willing to change and turn my life around
In agreement with all the restrictions
Even planning to follow though with my promise
I promised God in a prayer today
That I would try again to work with her
Going back to church when possible
And maybe even getting involved again
As hard as it is to describe what I'm feeling
I really doubt this has had time to sink in
And I anticipate things becoming more strange
Before and if they go back to normal

Losing

I'm losing the one thing I never had
The ability to drive at high speeds
Any violation of my sentence, however minor
Will land me back in front of the judge
And that means goodbye free world
Hello to jail and being raped
Taking a chance with this on the line
It totally out of the question
No more J-walking
No more littering
No more rolling stops
No more passing game
Take a different road
One in a reduced speed zone
Keeping in mind that only one
Mistake will end it all

Smart-Ass

Although at the time
The thought never entered my head
The commanding lady
Really misread me
Somehow this repetition

Talking down all day long
Made her lose the insight
To notice others at her level
Grinding in a point
To be hateful and mean is one thing
But trying to insult my intelligence
Normally, I would not stand for it

Week Two

Oh me, Oh my, week two
Yes I'm back at church again
After watching templars
Worship dead heads and demons
Back in the house of God
What a transition to make
When heading away from
National Geographic
Prayers I had were answered
Leaving me with no questions

Community Service

My exhaustion is visible
When I make the decision
To sit out and observe
The third consecutive aerobics class
Shoveling rocks and dirt
Into a wheel barrow
To be pushed and dumped repeatedly
For almost five hours
Has now become my routine
For 7:30AM each Saturday
Atleast the next twelve weeks
If it doesn't rain
I also picked up more work hours
54 paid hours weekly
Plus 4-5 unpaid
I'm left very unsure

How long I can do this
Of if like everything else
It will quickly become routine
Just another part of the hectic life
I try to maintain

Overeating

Next time I go through life's buffet
I'm not going to overfill my plate
I've yet to compromise my sleep
But many areas will be damaged
My balancing act
Becomes ever so more difficult
When Anne is home
And expects a majority of my time
Juggling work, church, community service
Wedding planning and pre-martial counseling
Paying off my monthly bill and debt
Yet still not speeding at all
I must remain careful
Walking on this thin ice for 12 months
Although in about three
My load will lighten considerably
The little things I enjoy doing
To put a smile on my face
Will begin to be the center
Of my limited universe
And making sure they occur
In this critical period
Will make a gigantic difference
In the final outcome

Hard Days

Some days are harder than others
Some time I have to walk away
Better a good example by absence
Than staying to fuel an argument
I am often left wondering
If this pen and this notebook
Are really getting out my feelings
Of if it's a convenient way to forget
During times like these I pray
For subtraction and not addition
To the bottled up anger
I am terrified will erupt…

Secret

No matter how many words I write
Even if you read them all
Regardless of how long you've "known" me
Or witnessed me after a fall
It doesn't matter how much I like you
If my emotions are nothing but love
Never will anyone have a free pass
Able to block or dodge me aside or above
This tremendous secret that I keep
Becomes harder to deal with day by day
And if I'm right about what just might happen
You'd do better to steer clear of my way
This pile of straw has been growing now
For more years than ever before
Long ago it should have broken my back
But I've locked it all behind a door
The key was tossed into an ocean
That I might forget this inner turmoil
But it calls to me wanted to come home
When my blood begins to boil
All the pressure from the whole world's weight
Is beginning to seep through the cracks
If enough of it escapes this closet

It will swallow me in its tracks

Fair

Sitting in a room filled with people
Who are brimming with mixed emotions
I concentrate on a nearby television
And try to become as a statue
Being careful to move as little as possible
To avoid eye contact at all costs
Most likely appearing as if I don't care
When it is so far from the truth
Disagreeing with almost every decision
Those who so ready for change tend to make
I can't help but feel I'm being selfish
Though my security blanket has also been removed
Just when things are beginning to look up
And my doubt of God's presence is vanishing
The world reminds me of the one constant
Nothing is or ever will be fair

Recorder

My recorder that has been so helpful
If only for the purpose of venting
When what I have to say is so inappropriate
I would not want another soul to hear
Now is primarily used to hear her voice
A daily reminder that someone loves me
That can be pulled out anytime I need it
And repeated causing me to smile forever
Such a simple device has been present
For decades with very few changes
And although I never wanted it before
It seems to have become a strong need
When I remove my coat it stays with me
While asleep it sits on my nightstand
At all times it's within my reach
This toy that brings me comfort

Anchor

I thought that getting over you
Would be just another piece of cake
But the memories we share are so strong
That like an anchor they hold me in place
Unable to set sail in the vast ocean
My defenses are lowered to almost nothing
And any pirate that sees me stranded
Is likely to take everything that remains
My self confidence is shattered
Day dreaming of the way things were
The only choice I have is to jump overboard
Swim to land and try to forget
Left wondering how I can feel this way
Each one I assume will just be another notch
On my pole of experiences and relationships
Leads me right back to where I started from
Creating a new ship to go back to sea
Hoping its anchor will not again be stuck
By some poor fool willing to take a chance
With whomever I have reinvented myself as this time

Time too slow?

Interesting how the only phrase
Heard from him up to his point
Regarding time in any manner or fashion
Was how fast it seemed to roll by
Apparently I never caught on
That in the down times this subject does not arise
Because speed is equated with happiness
And the lack thereof is equated with depression
Yesterday the statement finally changed
The day seemed to be taking way too long
Perhaps this is a new warning sign
To keep me on the tips of my toes
Not giving much thought to it

I continued on as planned
Trying to keep the two of us active
Perhaps missing other signals
Only soon to be told
That I treat him like a dog
Obviously untrue, yet hurtful
Maybe I learned a lesson

My recipe

A significant change is on the way
Effecting several aspects of my life
But I'm choosing what I now believe
To be the intelligent way to handle it
Not worrying until the last minute
Because I do not fully understand
And I need not waste time or energy
Consumed with another unknown
My usual recipe to deal with such things
Is to ignore them all together
Instead of contemplating "what ifs"
Just pretending it will stay as is

A test

I'm now being given
A golden opportunity
To cease the selfishness
And put someone else first
It seems much more likely
That God will listen
If my prayers are for others
And not about myself
Yet I wonder
How virtuous I really am
If this prayer is for us both
Or only for his well-being
Long after my plea is answered
I will still be left wondering

If I was being selfless
Or looking out for my own skin

A father

I don't enjoy watching
The misguided teachings
Of a father stuck in stereotypes

Thinking, speaking up, and taking control
Are primarily male attributes
And crying is forbidden

Using condescending comparisons
Repeatedly calling his son a two year old
For being less than perfect

How he can be so high and mighty
With his glaring speech impediment
Seems to escape me

But as usual in the case
It is not even my place
To share an idea or two

Just sit back and watch
As the two butt heads
Until one of them tires and gives up
For a few days

Can't it

Every time I hear the phrase
It can't get any worse than this
I shudder to imagine
How untrue the statement is
I can't believe
That I would have the nerve to say it
Even if I was covered by blood

And surrounded by lifeless bodies
At that point it could obviously get worse
Being caught, tried, convicted, incarcerated
Deciding to kill myself or getting the death penalty
Being locked in a crazy house forever
And all of that is only one example
Of how one particular situation could get worse
Most people who use this phrase
Are no where close to that situation
Not only does it seem to be tacky
But an open invitation for evil
To come knocking at your door
And ask you to sit down for a drink

Finally There

Talk about everything going to hell
My anger is so far past words
Retribution has taken over completely
And it needs to be swift and brutal
I care not about lessons learned
My only concern is punishment
But I should have known when I heard his words
"Today can't get any worse"
Well not unless you count verbal assault
Spitting, kicking, flailing, stomping
And throwing a brick through and into my car
I already turned the other cheek
When I called the police
It was not to protect me but hold me back
From committing murder on this asshole
With a ten year old mentality
I plan to just wash my hands clean
From the bleeding of cleaning up the glass
He left splattered throughout my car
And give him the ultimatum
Pay for all damages and my time
Or I press charges
And during those days in jail for breaking probation
A few rapes may clear his mind

Other Cheek

Last time I turned the other cheek
Somehow I managed to do it again
But this is not my personal philosophy
And I refuse to let anything change it
A person is given one opportunity to make a huge mistake
And in this case given two
But life then converts to a baseball game
Three strikes and you're out
If he so much as looks at me wrong
JAIL!
Hesitating to press charges
Left as I watched another window shatter
One of us is very lucky
I did not take him up on his offer to fight
Because we would both probably be in the hospital
And one of us may have been in a casket

My Test

God tested and measured me last week
And I was found unfit and unworthy
To be part of his congregation
To be one of his followers
I'm just another sinner
Who may never learn
Just what it takes to control my temper
In my head as well as my body
I decided to skip those services
Both Wednesday and Sunday last week
Because I just didn't feel right
About belonging to such a group
Somewhere in the Bible it says
That thinking something bad
Is equal to doing the deed
In that case I'm scared
I think the most horrid things

But somehow remain in just enough control
To walk away from the situation
Before I begin to explode

Put it in Dollars

How much is my sanity worth
And what about my patience
What is the price of my health
With a smile smeared on my face
Could someone please assign
A numeric amount I should expect
For endlessly giving to this people
And living in this time and place
I think that maybe pay per hour
Is greatly over-rated
And maybe the scale could go to minutes
To make it more worthwhile
The teachers I saw yesterday
Deserve at a very minimum
A million dollars an hour
To work in conditions oh so vile
I on the other hand don't usually mind
The way in which I am salaried
Except there is no way to tack on
The two minutes where I lose my head
Is that how it will always be
A great day followed by an abrupt ending
That leaves me wishing I had left
Early to avoid the certain dread

Todays Schools

Almost afraid to write
In my one-day job
Where I watch students
Constantly disrespect teachers
Forget about a paddle
Some of these *children*

Need a gun to their head
Just to pay attention
Yet others fallen through the cracks
Do exactly as they are told
Following instruction like robots
Finished with assignments in minutes
Yet I understand
Why no real discipline is used
When in this neighborhood
And in this city
Where nothing matters
The truth is obvious
No child left behind
Is complete nonsense
By virtue of leaving
Not a single one without school
They make everyone else suffer
And continue to bring down the system
That was created to help them
Not hurt them

Time on my hands

Although I've had
Much more time on my hands
I have been completely obsessive
About the situation
Until Yesterday
When I tried to remember
Why I was so angry
And what really happened
A person who could easily
Be locked up in a hospital
Without the understanding
Of what he was doing
Just another lost temper
Tempting me to lose mine
With a brick in my car
And spit in my face
Now not so pissed

I try to remember
What worked me up
And how I came down
Realizing I was more mad
That I was so close
To fighting back
Than I was at him

Stones

Sticks and Stones
May break my bones
But words
Can break my heart
So if you please
Don't talk to me
I would much rather
A fight you start
Your thoughts can stay
All tight locked up
Inside that empty sphere
We call a head
But when you begin
To open your mouth
I may stitch your lips shut
Zigzagged blood red thread

A wise decision

I could not decide
What to get him
For his birthday
From several options
But because we share interests
And enjoy the same things
I decided to get them all
Covering each of the bases
When the day came he arrived
Directed towards my room

Each possibility lain out before him
I simply asked him to choose
There were five in all
Four of which were new
And one I had owned a while
But it seemed to fit in
His choice was simple and almost immediate
Although he pretended to have difficulty
The only one not purchased just for him
Was that which he decided upon
Surprisingly happy I was
Not only that I was to keep the newer items
But that our tastes remained so similar
And the negative memory of that sword would leave with it

<u>My Boss</u>

If I finish writing this
Before my boss arrives
It means she does not follow
The motto of the boy scouts
I believe this from memory is right (A scout is…)
Trustworthy, loyal, helpful, friendly
Courteous, kind, obedient, cheerful
Thrifty, brave, clean, and reverent
I think all of that would imply
That they are also on time
But she has made the statement
That she is not a morning person
So I'm not expecting too much
It seems to me that qualified or not
A supervisor should lead by example
That never seems to happen
Not just here
So please don't get me wrong
I can recall very few
Who actually followed the rules
And asked one to do as they do
Not do as they say
And each and every time

Leaving me full of dismay

The kids

Sitting in teachers seats
Playing online video games
Not respect for anyone
Especially themselves
Attention seeking
But for what purpose
Boisterous outbursts
With no reason
Problem numero uno
They talk too much
And they never shut up
But they should

Trading Places

By my definition trading places
Would resemble many popular movies
My mind and my soul somehow transferred
Into a body I was unfamiliar with
Having to assume all responsibility
Of something one is totally unaccustomed to
An entire lifestyle, family, and friends trade off
While pretending to be someone you're not
This seems it could be advantageous
To two opposite people who want a change
Like a bed-ridden person with a good mind
And a busy-body who needed a vacation
Even if each desperately wanted
What the other person got to experience
Realistically the shock could almost kill you
Likely quickly growing weary missing the routine
For me this one doesn't take any thinking
But then again I already consider myself happy
If I had been dealt a different hand
Then I suppose the thought would arise

113

Trading Problems

Would I ever take the chance
To trade problems with someone else
Maybe if I fully understood
What I was getting myself into
I would also have to be facing
One heck of some bad problems
In my own life that were worse
Than anything I have even encountered yet
Obviously the way one views a "problem" is subjective
And would most likely depend on the circumstances
Which in no way could be the same
If only trading problems and not places
So it seems that yes I would trade problems
Perhaps only for a temporary basis
My thinking being, a different point of view
Can be all that's needed for answers

Magic Lamp

How much would you pay
If magic lamps were for sale
To uncomplicated things
Only one wish per lamp
Perhaps two different types
One where wishes effect only you
And the other effecting everyone
But is that separation possible
If we are all connected
And work together to form a society
Which works with other groups
To make the world turn
I have to think no
A wish would be universal
So then how much should it cost
And where should the money go
Should applicants be screened

By a committee like the UN
To approve the wish in advance
So no tyrant could ruin it all
Could anyone really understand
The infinite possibilities and repercussions
Only one simple wish could make
In our current way of life
Maybe these questions are the reason
That magic lamps do not exist
And if one ever materialized
God would be forced to intervene

Back to Normal

Things have fallen back in place
Perhaps best to just forget about last Tuesday
Soon I will have what I didn't know I missed
The free time to relax, sleep, and pray
For now I try my best to focus
On all the good coming full speed
That seems to have no visible ending
And that ending is something I don't need
My routine can continue as it was
Before the mess got me ever so near
To losing my temper with more than words
And unleashing that which I most fear
No idea do I have what perfect is like
Nor will I until my time here is through
But I'm grateful that life's back to normal
And it's tint is no longer so blue

Autumn

I honestly believe that you
Were one of the few people
That believed much as I do
There's no such thing as normal
So from the moment we met
Until the most recent goodbye

You've always treated me as just a person
Never above or below anyone else
It could have been our similar tastes
In friends, music, and how we dressed
But I refuse to believe mere coincidence
Made us bond and stay friends
It was likely no secret I thought
You were adorable from day one
But let us face the brutal reality
I find all nice women attractive
What you may have forgotten
Was how you introduced me
To the movie Halloween
And it continues to be my favorite
When it gets the time of year
That the leaves all start to fall
And perhaps forever I will think of you
Every time someone names the season

A good week gone bad

This was my birthday week
It should have been full of cheer
But right now I sit at home
And wish I could stomach a beer
Instead I go for the liquor
Which disguised with coke
Doesn't taste so bad
When mixed and going for broke
I took a few of this pill
And a few more of that
Perhaps I will just take a long nap
Perhaps just end up another stat
Right now I really don't care
And I just don't understand
How things could be going so good
And then just sink into quicksand
Barely awake and breathing
I decide to write these lines
Maybe someone will hear me

And pick up on the signs
I don't think I'm quite suicidal
But I'm gradually working my way there
Would be nice to have something to hug
Maybe my giant blue Carebear
By the minute I'm getting more exhausted
What happens when you use this mix
Of Klonopin, Ibuprofen, Benedryll and alcohol
To solve the problem you need to fix
I've turned off my cell phone for now
So no use trying to stall
Hopefully I will wake up tomorrow
And realize this was just call
For the help I so desperately need
To make it even one more day
If anything goes wrong tomorrow
On this earth I may not stay

Bored

I think that the graveyard
Would be more entertaining
Slaving for hours
For nothing but freedom
Than this paid assignment
To observe in a school
Where the children are monsters
Are there are no cages
Time is creeping by
And the golden silence
Only increases my curiosity
Why am I here
One thing I'm now sure of
I could not be a teacher
Ignoring what I hear
Of paying attention
Either way the class becomes
A gigantic disruption
Where learning is impossible
And education is extinct

Too much to ask

I want to keep a job that I enjoy
With a schedule that is workable
Enough time left to rest and relax
Is that too much to ask?
I would like to renew my faith in God
After a lapse that's lasted ten years
To feel his warmth deep in my heart
Is that too much to ask?
I imagine myself soon to be married
Off on a wonderful honeymooner's trip
Seeing things and places I've never imagined
Is that too much to ask?
I pray for someday a son or daughter
And a wonderful and supportive family
For them to grow up healthy and happy
Is that too much to ask?
I enjoy now and for eternity will
Be thankful for my growing community
Of friends that would not turn their backs on me
Is that too much to ask?
I believe it is fair and I'm aware
That these requests are nothing short of selfish
But I also think it's just on the brink
Of being too much to ask

Thea

When we met you were but an acquaintance
And I likely seemed like an annoyance
But now after four years without a word
You sent an invitation to renew our friendship
The number of times I have thought of you
Grasping the one and only picture I have
With the two of us smiling at homecoming
And remembering the good times we shared
You borrowing my plaid pants for a few weeks
Get togethers at several of your apartments
And one that could have well been my last memory

On the New Years eve of two thousand
When I had idiotically mixed so many drugs
That my pupil's black filled the blue of my eyes
All those present were fearful for my survival
Many like you requesting I call back safe from home
I never knew how much I missed you
Until you chose the perfect time to contact me
This week has so far truly been a one eighty
When compared to the lack of light over the past few
Friendship is the one thing I have been missing
Since long before my late graduation
And to get such a gift for my birthday
May once again bring tears of joy to my eyes

Audrey

To the woman who
Became my basis of comparison
From the time I met her
Until the day I met Anne
I hope she finds
Everything she's looking for
And much more on her trip
To distant lands across the sea
Known probably the least time
Of most of my college friends
She found a special spot
To stay in my heart forever
With no one else
Have I ever been willing
To drop everything and everyone
Just for a few seconds with her
I find it difficult to believe
She may not be at my wedding
But we both have a lifetime
To develop and maintain our friendship

Christiane

On the very first day
Of even orientation
I met a soon to be
Best friend for life
Playing a silly game
Which I usually abhor
Having to do with knowing names
And throwing around a ball
Close her out of simplicity
Our names were one and the same
I discovered she lived across the hall
And enjoyed watching Blue's Clues
Such became our daily routine
While we laughed about her roommate
Later together discovered Casinos
And the wonder of Cherokee
She showed me how to juggle
And her infinite desire
To attend clown college someday
Showed me how to stick with a goal
Since school I have not seen her
But I know someday I will
And we can share smiles and laughs
At stores as the years have passed

Runaway

Now when I hear Soul Asylum
"Runaway train never coming back"
I will think only of him
In prayer that he will show up
Feeling it was almost my discovery
That he wasn't at school
Didn't get off the bus
And failed to be at the neighbors
I stayed with his father
Tried to help make appropriate phone calls
And returned to look for three hours
Through the thickets and woods
How can someone so young

With no money and no means
To survive on his own
Be hiding in the woods
He's afraid of the dark!
And his dad remains emotionless
At least appears that way to me
Maybe the guilt and fear
That his son may be gone forever
Has not quite set in
Or he hides it very well

Survival

Scrambling through the woods
Calling out his name
Following after every sound
Wishing things could be the same
Finding footprints in the mud
Leading me to nowhere
Flashing pictures left and right
No one has seen him there
Could I possibly handle
Being in his position
Outside two consecutive nights
No clothes and no nutrition
I grew up a boy scout
Where the least I would expect
Was a tent, a fire, and some food
And someone to direct
At this point I hope he has
Broken into someplace dry and warm
When the rain begins to pour
He'll need shelter from the storm

Alison

She can be credited with
My re-introduction to some music
Like Paula Abdul and Counting Crows

And an ear to always listen
Always one of the most stable
Having her man from then till now
Many classes we shared together
And many study groups we helped one another
Of all my college friends
I talk with her the most
And feel our friendship has expanded
Rather than deflated like a flat tire
Never judgmental
Sometimes needing assurance
That decisions though difficult were correct
And everyone can't always be happy
Trying her hardest to a degree
To put everyone else before her
Lessons I learned I will not forget
Gullible and yet so mature
If I had taken a different path
I might have been so lucky
Because although I am gullible
I am far from her in learning

Kira and Megan

Although I try to think
A lesson is always learned
After a whole book written for you
I now feel I was un-burned
In retrospect you two were so tiny
And as pain does, it faded
Refusing to change from being me
I'm still open and not jaded
Maybe now a bit slower
When opening up to a stranger
The reality now is you were nothing
My life you could never endanger
I don't think I will forget you
But it's long since time to move along
At last I can just forgive you
All us three immature and wrong

U

You played me like a beginner
Knew exactly what to say
To get me to buy you some liquor
Invisible leash leading the way
Plenty of sex appeal was it
Nothing more and nothing less
Then maybe three days later
In a friends arm you were caressed
Glad there was never a date
And that we will never be in touch
Couldn't salvage even a friendship
But I didn't want one much
You defined user so clearly
That I've managed to stay away
From those people who never act
But always have something to say

Amber

You were likely the friend
Who finally made me understand
Nothing visible is all that important
When it comes to companionship
Not the way it should have been
I never took you to see my friends
Never grasping how wonderful you were
Until it was too late and you moved
Then delusional I tried to replace you
Living in the fantasy world that
All full figured women would be nice
How stupid could I be?
After my heart was trampled over
Numerous more time than I care to count
I finally gained the knowledge
I had been force-fed but regurgitated my whole life
Love is not in the smile or eyes
It's not in the hips or the chest
It can't be determined by weight or height

And really has nothing to do with sight
Physical Attraction is great
And a healthy led life is too
But in the end it's the person inside
That determines if the love is true

A Desent Day

It Seems like today
Might finally go as planned
No out of whack behaviors
And no totally strange demands
Write myself a few words
Get to eat my normal lunch
Watch my soap called Days
Then get to shop a bunch
Make a little detour
To Bestbuy® so I can see
The exorbitant prices
On video camera for me
Then out to the bowling lanes
For some strikes or a spare
If today is really this easy
Then paying me won't be fair
But then again after all that
Drive for a two hour sit
Listening to someone talk
About a bunch of shit just kidding
Wanting a confession his son admit
Then its off to home sweet home
To watch my name is Earl
Maybe do a little paperwork
And dream of my favorite girl

Separate

How is it I accomplish
Separation of work and home
The harder I try to do it

The further away I roam
Simple breathing or a game
Does not change my focus
And no magician can wave a wand
With a simple hocus pocus
It's like I'm locked inside a room
Without even a door
And to escape I must just write
Until my hand is sore
When at last I don't succeed
And I tire of trying
I put away my pen and pad
And to sleep I go all crying
If a stranger to my plight
You might think I am lying
But if my mental state was visible
You'd see that I am dying

Untitled

My memory is failing me in such a way
That a short cut ends up the long way around
I have no idea where I'm bound
Mile markers, road signs, and other frames of reference
Slowing become blurry as I drift along the street
Maybe only steps, just a few more feet
But not knowing where I'm going or where I've been
Leaves me clueless so I continue to walk
Wishing someone had the time to talk
Continuing, I occasionally see chalk outlines
Curious and wondering if this was a joke
If not what were the last words they spoke
As I keep walking everything begins to get hazy
Eventually all the faces become one and the same
And they are just like me, As I forget my own name
Just another mindless zombie continuing
Trying to be unique and looking for a fix
To escape this never ending matrix

Emily

Phone ringing but not expected
After glancing at the time I answer
Immediately upon hearing the voice
Several pounding questions being to surface
If this is who they say it is
Why the hell are you calling me
I'm nothing more than a fading memory
Long ago caught in the web you spun
Another question I would like you to answer
Is why at this hour are you calling
When most people, even Americans, would be asleep
And it's likely my happy dream could have continued
Now I'm surely going to continue
Thinking about these questions and more
Long after your pointless need to cry for attention
Has been met and you're sound asleep
I wonder would you think it was worthwhile
If you realized it takes more than some fling
Reminding me with shock-filled statements
Of why we were never anything
You are only memorable in a negative way
Because you represent my fall from grace
The first time I cheated in a relationship
And how terrible everyone but you felt
At that time you did not care
And now I deserve the right
To reciprocate the favor you gave me
"Goodnight!" *hangs up the phone*

Two People

Two people I know
Keep breaking the rules
Neither quite understands
That they look like fools
Both have one thing in common
On that I'm as sure as can be
They only act out with those they love

126

But their so called friends never see
How different things could turn out
If I took a video camera along
Recording how they misbehave
Showing them how they are wrong
Letting everyone in on the secret
That their warped minds believe
Our love is really unconditional
When in reality, they can't achieve
There is no such thing as unconditional love
It is a total fool's fairy tale
There is at least one action anyone can do
To make any relationship fail

That list

When I tried to remember
And add each to a list
Of all the females I have dated
At first it made me pissed
So many mistakes
Lessons learned the hard way
Just looking for that one
To love me back and stay
But now when I consider
The few friends of them that remain
That hold on to a piece of my heart
I can wipe away the stain
Left here by the vast majority
Of the bad and useless wastes of time
I could count the good up on one hand
And to me that lessens the crime
The majority of women I've respected
Achieved the simple title of friend
A different love I share with them
And will continue until the end

Dearborn

I always hear about the guys
Bragging about who they had
In bed with them the night before
And at dawn threw out making them sad
Well this girl put them all to shame
After she used me I was to find
She had a reputation for one night stands
And apparently I was just blind
Needed not sweet poetry
A few drinks and a wink of her eye
I was wrapped around her finger
And in less than an hour she said goodbye
No returned phone calls, not even hello
When I saw her on campus by day
But when I mentioned her name to friends
I realized this was just her way

Blue

The sky has a gradual fade in
Starting almost orange and purple
Then from a very light blue
Back to above my head
Here it's black
There is no color
It's as if I'm separated
In another world
Ever changing until
All the lighter shades
Switch over to darkness
And only man-made light remains
Here is where I feel most safe
Surrounded by a blanket of nothing
Not knowing what will happen next
Disguising even the most obvious
Relying more on a sence of sound
Than on my mere vision
And as the world turns round
Light returns in a backwards sky

Still feeling

Still feeling half asleep
I make an obvious effort
To make it though another day
The stress is overwhelming
In an attempt to relax yesterday
I took a few benedryl for sleep
But of course I slept wrong
On my back creating neck pain
Now I am not only tired and cranky
But my neck has a reduced range of motion
In such a hurry last night
I did not wash my bathing suit
The hot tub could work wonders
Towards loosening me up
And relieving this awful pain
That I can't get used to

Asleep

My mind is still asleep
But I am physically awake
Somewhere between dreams and life
How did I make this mistake?
Propping up my head now
Maybe my only escape
If only I could fix myself
With glue and masking tape
But that would be too easy
And life is no piece of cake
Still I have severe doubts
On how much more I can take

Known

I don't know what this is about
Maybe that's why it's such a scare
I can't tell if I should be happy or sad

All I know is it hits me there
Right in my heart and in my soul
Where the risk is ever more great
That no barriers will be thick enough
And it will permeate
Through my defenses so easily
Like a warm knife cutting butter
So worked up I am right now
I can't make sense of the clutter
All my levels rising up
Like a train whistle about to blow
Not only am I unsure what will help me
I have doubts even God would know
If She did would She help me along
Or am I walking all alone
Desperately needing a sign or signal
To decided to make itself known

The Salem open

Well it was fun while it lasted
My home away from home
Where I was considered a champion
Despite my average performance
My record still stapled to the wall
Twenty One stokes below par
And thirty-four $10 bull's-eyes
The lowest score on any Friday
Today they will likely be trashed
And most memories I've shared
Will be left in a few putters
And the trophies in my room
What else could occupy so much time
Be completely free and go with work
When I find the answer to that
It will probably cease to matter
Already renewing my interests
In video games and movies
I still have over fifty coupons
Never to be redeemed

Kerri

Since high school only closer
Had the two of us become
She saw me at my worst
And also at my best
Then finally came a boyfriend
And I figure she would be happy
But I'll never know
Because she discarded me
No phone calls in so long
I no longer remember the number
And enough messages left
To fill up ten voicemail boxes
What I did, probably nothing
And I assume I'll never know
Unless I run into her by chance
Still noticing her glow
So much time has passed now
I would not recognize
Her clothes, her hair, her smile
If she looked me in the eyes

Softball

I equivocate this sport with evil
After all the problems I have had
Between myself and the love of my life
With announcers, family and friends I overhear
Your sister isn't even playing!
She's a bench warmer with a broken foot
Wake from this idiotic dream
Where she will be a part of the team
The crazy coach has no idea
What is fair and what is right
Just rotating the same nine players
While the others resist the right
Parents should unite with signatures

And letter for the school dean
And if that fails to work
Grab some bats and be mean

President Doosh

Talking faster does not help
Not does improper inflection
Repetition makes you look silly
Take a look at your own reflection
When you say "next question please"
Or blame it on the Democrats
Refuse to veto a single bill
Take a look at the poll stats
The war is totally asinine
Be a parent and teach by example
Get things in your own country straight
Before you try ideas on a test sample
Iraq does not want democracy
The want us to get the hell out
The sooner this happens I can feel
Like I no longer have to shout
Each dead person from both sides
Their blood it is on your hands
Please stop all your senseless lying
Before impeachment we all demand

Nerves

Already trying my nerves
By asking before it is time
To have the next cigarette
I wish it was a crime
The chimney of you burns hot
Fire lasting less than a minute
But the smell as usual follows
Oh God what a horrible scent
All these so called friends
Role models, family, and workers

Daily encouraged you to quit
But it just doesn't matter
You don't care what we think
You don't care what we say
As long as in the end
You get things your own way
Beginning to see your darker side
And how you really tick
The methods you use to trick us
Yet someone I am not sick
This undying faith in myself
That I can someone help create change
Keeps me coming back for more daily
Instead of a life rearrange

Letting it out

Before the anger compounds again
I've decided to release it
Let these words serve as my weapon
And this paper as its target
If I knew I could not be caught
And life would remain the same
Besides the guilt I'm bound to feel
I might go a little insane
First decided which of my swords
Or if to use them all
Sharpen each to a razor tip
Decide who deserves to fall
Upon the realization
That no one fits the description
Push the morality out of my head
And murder with no discrimination
At times I wonder if my conscience
Would really devour my soul
Or if I could just shrug it off
Flip the switch back in control
Move on pretending all was fine
And that I could not hurt a fly

At least now I wrote it down
So no one has to die

Interruption

I typically hate interruptions
Especially to my daily routine
But this one was an exception
As horrible as it might seem
Someone close (a daughter) to a friend of mine
Has passed from earth's pain and sorrow
Although she goes to a better place
It may take too long for tomorrow
Now it's time to put life on hold
And gather up with the family
Without forgetting what has happened
To focus on all the good memories
Today I ask all that read this
Send thoughts and prayers her way
You need not even know her name
God is with her today

A Bad night

This discussion that has been brewing in my head
Over and over constantly becoming larger
Had to reach its popping point
The night before she left on vacation
So many ridiculous and stupid statements
Wishing I had a redo and could reverse time
Wondering why on that day and that time
That it all came out like a landslide
But we talked, began to cuddle, watch TV
Everything would end up okay, maybe
She fell asleep leaning on me missing the ending
To the show she suggested that we record and watch
I did not really notice she was out
Until my loud mouth did the trick again
Realizing at the turning point what was going on

I blurted out a self hoorah for myself
She awoke confused at first, then realizing it was over
Asking me why I let her fall asleep in the first place
I fumbled through excuses and offered to rewind
She had only been out for a measly five minutes
The charged energy from before came back to us both
After the night could have turned out somewhat nice
Being stubborn, as she is, she refused my offer
I slammed the controller yelling "Fuck This" and went to bed
After she did in fact watch the five minutes she came to bed
I was cold and did not acknowledge her
We both fell asleep, mostly likely me a lot quicker
And the next morning we pretended as if nothing happened

Beginning AA

Without reading more
Than a quick summary
And the forward of the book
I begin my journey inward
Casting out my many obvious flaws
Attempting to really get in touch with God
Stepping myself from the judgments
Perhaps most difficult, listening without interruption
My being manic this is indescribably hard
My favorite past time is talking
To my best friend for the 1000th time
Or to a stranger or newcomer
I insist on beginning the never-ending story
All autobiography, with occasional twists
To each and every person I meet
Really, I should just write a book!
But it never ceases or desists
Regardless of the shrinks or the meds
Not to mention family and my friends
And the countless people I've lost
Further into the book I may learn
The secret to unlocking my emotions
On a psychical level while sending the glue
To keep my mouth shut long enough to listen

My first Chip

Yesterday I attended an AA meeting
I have been before
But not to a meeting group
That relied on the 12-step book
Others were always too large
And too many attention seekers
Just wanting to explore
Their last huge binge drinking episode
this was much smaller
Mostly late middle aged people
And the book was important!
Step six was the topic
If you are not a member
Or forget that step
Summed up it says
Allowing God to take away your character defects
This hit me like a ton of bricks
The more sharing
The more I seemed intrigued
To the point where I shared
Still feeling the need to be me
I told an anecdotal story
Causing everyone to laugh out loud
But I felt a powerful charge
Many statements like
Sometimes you just have to keep your mouth shut
Rang so true
That I accepted my first chip

Ironic

I now have the proof
To back up my words
The promises and convictions
I've long self prophesied
To the doubters and fakers
Who pretended to understand
Secretly thinking behind closed doors
"He" could never do that
Well I did!
And justified, I would again
But it's ironic how the unleashed hell
Was so totally unjustified
No reason under the sun
Just pent up frustration
And a lack of ways
For a healthy release
Now I stare down these thoughts
Meeting them face to face
Trying to change myself
Discovering the difficulty
I never changed anyone else
And although they say it's impossible
Right now it seems nothing
Compared to working on me
Doubting anything will work
Besides continuous repetition and example
Left curious how many decades
Until I budge an inch

Becoming what I hate

The one thing I could never stand
Is someone that could be called a hypocrite
Now this term does apply to nearly everyone
But I mean a boastful hypocrite
The type of person who would preach
Giving a good message to the crowds
Immediately turning around to do the opposite

137

At some point realizing it and not caring
Today was the point I realized it
But I do sincerely care
My statement and preaching about friendships
How they dwindle with lack of communication
My general rule, call or write a few times
If no response then write them off
Erase # and address from phone and paper
And go on as if they don't exist
Somehow I neglected all my internet friends
Besides the ones who wrote me
Just getting lost in my own private world
No longer emailing or posting hellos
I've become what I hate most
Ignoring those who've been there for me
And giving all my attention
To the newest interest
Like a child with a new toy
I drop all the others
Forgetting what they represent and where they came from
And just move on aimlessly

Comfortable

Now that most of the lifting
And rearrangement of furniture is done
Relaxation has again become a state of mind
Instead of a rare occasional circumstance
We are very much elated and loving
And the past few weeks seem distant
Similar my previous home from forever
Lunches even partially made for me
Dinner is ready when I get home
Dishwasher takes care of all the mess
My routine life is getting back in order
But as usual a few things I forget
There are not always please and thank you
Spouted from my lips for all she does
Not intentionally I am an asshole
Forgetting how wonderful little gestures can be

Center of Attention

What happens when someone
Who needs to constantly be
The center of attention
Doesn't get their way
If you're really that curious
Switch places with me for a day
You may find yourself caught
In a no win situation
Where being friendly or quiet
Does not get the job done
The explosion is imminent
Imagine polar opposite of fun
Things could stay okay for minutes
Hours, days, and even more
then purposely self-aggravates
Saying life is such a bore
Disagree and you might be attacked
So be sure you think before
You act

Guts

Do I have what it takes
To stand up in front of strangers
And just ask for a simple prayer
When I know it should be done
How far along am I
To being truly grown up
Now 27 years
But the fear remains
What could really happen
Crying?...it would be good
I've been trying for years
Without a bit of success
A tremble in my voice
So do half of the people

Who even try to talk
Even the president
Not that he's a good example
But surely if W' can give a speech
I can say a few words
To a supportive group
Tonight we will see
Will I put a mic in my hands
Or sit quietly in the back
Without the guts or glory

Relief

Relief is the only word
That comes into my mind
When they found my missing friend
We tried so hard to find
I sincerely hope
The lesson learned
And all his points are made
Because if not
I fear the next time
His health will surely fade
Glad that we can talk again
Things back to status quo
How can I help him realize
To just follow his life's flow
If he doesn't
He'll be gone
With a marker left behind
For a boy
Who was searching
For something he could not find

Finished

Maybe now I'm done
Writing about that part of my past
I can begin to write about the present
And the things that truly last
My current friendships that matter
And my romance everlasting
I have too much to be happy for
To focus on the past obsessing
Today could be a landmark
To stop the inner dialogue
All of the what if's
To rise above this hazy fog
Think of the now and future
My family and how it will grow
How lucky I am today
To realize this and know
That part one of life is finished
And part two wants to surge
Push over the old and make room
For a happy me to emerge

Letting it Out

Before the anger compounds again
I've decided to release it
Let these words serve as my weapon
And this paper as its target
If I knew I could not be caught
And life would remain the same
Besides the guilt I'm bound to feel
I might go a little insane
First decide which of my words
Or if to use them all
Sharpen each to a razor tip
Decided she deserved to fall
Upon the realization
That no one fits the description
Push the morality out of my head

And murder with no discrimination
At times I wonder if my conscience
Would really devour my soul
Or if I could just shrug it off
Flip the switch to back in control
move on pretending all was fine
And that I could not hurt a fly
At least now I wrote it down
So no one has to die

Interruption

I typically hate interruptions
Especially to my daily routine
But this one was an exception
As horrible as it might seem
Someone close to a friend of mine
Has passed from earth's pain and sorrow
Although she goes to a better place
It may take too long for tomorrow
Now is time to put life on hold
And gather up with the family
Without forgetting what has happened
To focus on all the good memories
Today I ask all that read this
Send thoughts and prayers her way
You need not even know her name
God is with her today

Anniversary Poem

Well today is the day
You've made it 34 months
How anyone can put up with me
That long is amazing
No one has ever done it besides family
You're the first and only
And the past two weeks alone
Were enough to scare away lifelong friends

Most amazing perhaps
Is the way you continue
To tell me more and more
How much you love me
Long ago I gave up
On soul mates and first sight love
But you've broken the mold
On how wonderful love can be
Never once pressured me
To change a single thing
Despite my constant suggestions
Trying to force you to change
To stick up for me
To be angry at your family
Age never had anything to do with it
You're far more mature than me
I cherish you first
Above all else in this earth
And I hope several years from now
I can help you to give birth

(Obviously in conception, not in the process)

My pen

There are times when I am happy
I don't have access to this pen
This way of exhausting my emotions
Into stanzas of hate and disgust
The picture I paint for the world
May be of butterflies and flowers
But underneath it's all unbearable pain
Ripping at my soul for release
How I chose to focus the energy
Really makes no difference
As long as it's not inward
I will continue to smile
At times the pen is dangerous
Because the emotion has taken over
Anger breathing the thousands of walls

I've purposely buried it behind
There are short cuts for it to get out
Backdoors, certain statements open up
The "thinking first" aspect melts away
And I just belt out what's in my head
Usually next is regret and apologies
Force me back into a limbo
Where I stay until things are fixed
But nothing ever gets fixed

Threat?

Some would call it a threat or a promise
Indicating some law has been broken
I personally think of it as more of a suggestion
The simple statement "Don't fuck with me"
There is no "if, then" clause
No suggestions of a penalty are mentioned
Maybe an idea most people don't contemplate
Talking to me or being a friend doesn't mean you "know" me
Until you've experienced the full rage
And wrath of my temper
In my eyes you're merely an acquaintance
So I live in a world of acquaintances
When someone knows me completely
One of the two of us will be dead
I'll be locked up in prison or an asylum
And this writing will ring true
To be perfectly honest
I hope it never comes to that
I am perfectly content
Living a lie that never ends

Harmony

Finally Sunday night hit
And getting along seemed easy
We relaxed and watched TV
Before playing a short game
Then off to bed where some new thoughts
Were devised to keep her in the bed
Instead of over the edge
Both of us in the middle
The next morning was the 1st good sleep
She had gotten in weeks
No longer sick, too stressed
Or lying beside a drunk snoring fiancée
Yesterday went better than planned

Beard

Growing a beard
Not really my way
Fishing for attention
What will others say
If I am praised
Good chance it will stay
If I am scorned
It will go away
And just one comment
That I look gay
Will likely raise fists
In jail to decay
Now I've begun
Merry month of May
And nothing will fit here
That rhymes with A

Hump Day

Today is Wednesday
For a Monday to Friday worker, hump day

Halfway done
And almost weekend
The stress cycle made a U-turn
But got stuck in the middle
Neither work or personal is well
But I must keep on going
On one hand Anne is slipping
No computer, studying, exams, graduation
On the other is my dedication to work
New schedules, clients, beginnings, and endings
Three more days and half will be gone
And soon thereafter maybe all
Back to a memory I fondly remember
Without dreading each moment
Anne home, exams and graduation complete
And the computer fixed up for free
Job searching will begin or continue
And nights maybe we can relax
At work things will settle
They have to, hopefully new measures taken
Until next month
When the next change occurs

Going too far

If I had pre-thought it through
It would not be justified
But at least I could have called it
Some sort of payback for her behavior
After graduation we reached the hotel
And the drinking commenced
Half a bottle of rum, and a bottle of champagne later
I was smoking cigars and publicly urinating
She gave up on me and went to bed
And her father and his friend kept up subtle encouragement
SO many words came out that were private
Things I long ago promised not to share
I got sick after the cigar
I had no business trying to smoke
Knowing this would lead to the sickness

146

I kept going despite discouragement
1, 2, 3, 10 upchucks later we called it a night
I got in the bed after using heavy mouthwash
Five minutes later it was back to the bathroom
Another sick episode and I did not even clean the sink
In fact I fell over without any balance and made my way to the bed
Pushed away and no kisses offered
As my breath stank of smoke, alcohol, and vomit
I fell asleep alone
The next day my head pounded
We had to pull over for medicine
And I only wanted sleep
But I helped unpack for my new life

Better Off

Once again I'm better off
Just keeping my mouth shut
But I think I may understand
Because I bring out the emotions
She is hiding from the world
In order to make others happy
She sacrifices herself
Putting on a fake smile
I'm trying to prepare
For that day when it must end
When I am asked to leave
And to never return
Could be today, a week, a year
But eventually my charm will erode
Leaving only the real me
Perhaps that is not enough
Thinking you fixed one problem
Another pops up in its place
And this never ending cycle
Just a definition of life

Moving Out/Graduation

Talk about a bitch
Nothing was what she wanted
Her father had the right idea
Sitting on a sofa out of sight
That day finally got to the worst point
And started to move upward
Little did I expect or know
She had already made up her mind
Tomorrow would be worse
Starting okay with her parents
When she practiced walking
We talked and ate breakfast
Then the language started
Not that her dad doesn't speak the same way
But her mother never does anything wrong
She is so sweet and she was pleading
Finally I put my foot down
No kisses, no hugs, no ring, no apartment
If one more word so much as squeaked out
I can't take family arguments
Unless I am part of the family
Which I am at this point not
She ignored my promises and threats
And continued to use the language
I was happy when she left to talk
Happy for a break from her mouth
Excited this nightmare was almost over
I smiled eagerly as she walked the stage
That night I gave her a graduation present early
One that she would never forget
And then I regretted not going with my instinct
Leaving early before the party got going
So sloshed I was ignoring her
With champagne and rum I got sickly intoxicated
Getting sick repeatedly and pissing in public
I even tried to smoke a cigar
I suppose you could call it payback
But the information I divulged to her parents that night

Was much worse than the bad language she used
And is likely going to take a long time to get over

Moving In

Well it was not what I expected to say the least
Nothing in the place was as new as I had hoped
My request to forward my mail is taking 10 business days
And my old as hell refrigerator doesn't have an ice maker
The sink leaks, the doors stick, my requests are overlooked
But at least the first month's rent is free
That has to count for something
I love my new digital cable and high speed internet
And agreed about disagreeing, but not nicely
We argued to the point we were both ready to walk
Nothing could go exactly where either of us wanted
But with time, just a week, things are settling
It is beginning to feel like a home, however slowly
After 27 years in that house adjusting is hard
I do like the extra bedroom/computer/storage space
And the large closets and clean bathrooms are a plus
She is taking a week off work to get it set up
Whatever she chooses will be just fine with me
I just want it all unpacked and organized
The first night home cooked meal made a good impression
And after all the problems in the last two weeks
Things are getting back to normal and balance was at hand
If things could stay like this for eternity
I would always remain satisfied

Grandmother is here

Well I see Grandma
Which means one of the two things
Either her son or granddaughter
Is somewhere in the building
These run-ins I hate
Even with just family
Who may have forgotten me

But whom I never forget
Memories of the pathetic excuse
For what I called a relationship
Up until I opened my eyes
Stab at me like spears
If one of all must be chosen
As a complete regret
To be undone and rewound
I think it would be her

Passed Out

More and more commonly
Especially on Monday nights
I fall asleep accidentally
Without a goodnight phone call
In just a week
It will not be a concern
With her lying beside me
it will be obvious
No more problems
With cell phones not ringing
And messages not being delivered
Or worry about families
Just a look
to convey the exhaustion
And then off to bed
Without morning guilt

E

Two people never see the same situation
In anywhere near the same light
Moments away from what could have been beautiful
Or what could have been a big mistake
The time expired and we had to stop
Saying our goodbyes for the holiday
During that break my mind never once wondered
From the excitement and joy she had brought me

When I got back she was not to be found
And when found was always too busy
One weekend apart had transformed her outgoingness
Into an avoidance as if I had the plague
Never was I given an explanation
But at the time, could I have expected one?
Most likely another drug induced afterthought
That eroded as quickly as it started

Don't talk to me

I never expected the words
To be enunciated from her lips
"You'd probably do better not talking to me today"
My perception left YOU as the key word
If only I were really a part
Of this totally unpleasant group
Instead of a part-time addition
Understanding now to leave work at work
But I already would have given up
Lost all hope for a normal existence
Retrieved a sharp knife from the kitchen table
And run a very warm bath
Even in this act if I was a real part
Not much would change
They have seen it all ten times over
Never able to make the obvious change

Eyes

When I think of all the things
A human eye is unequipped to see
It reminds me of how little of reality
We actually get to experience
If more parts of our brains worked
We might be seeing ghosts in graveyards
We could be seeing demons roaming the earth
And have so many more explanations
The voices "Crazy" people hear

May actually be audible to everyone
And that person has only unlocked
A new spectrum of existence

Rocks

I put my good luck rocks
Back into my pants pocket
And try to force myself
To imagine any impact they will have
Not only good or bad luck
But even if I will remember
That they are in my pocket
Or notice their weight
Probably not
They might get washed
Forgetting to empty my pockets
Before I disrobe tonight
Through several rinse and wash cycles
They will get free and make noise
But they will have become bad luck rocks
For the appliances at home

Lady I know 2

Just as confused as before
I'm back on the park bench
No progress has been made
But none lost either
Never-ending is an oval
Round and round it goes
When will he stop walking
This nobody knows
Music blaring in headphones
Taking him away from this place
Far to planet space
Where no one knows his face
He is not a criminal
Not even in trouble

When it takes ten thousand years
To just walk a block
Because so many people are there
So many who do not care

Luck

Today my necklace broke
You know the one
I always wear it
Anne's class ring dangles from it
Well today I heard a clink
And immediately saw her ring
Doesn't appear damaged
But where is the chain?
After a few moments
Of groping my own neck and chest
I made a swift shake
And to the floor it fell
I believe in good luck
And typically in the last years
Bad things tend to happen
When I forgot this ring
So I placed it on my finger
My right ring finger
I know I won't lose it
But will it get stuck?
Summer is on the way
And my flesh will expand
I may get to find out
If soap can get a ring off
But for now it's kind of nice
Getting used to a ring
That I always wear on my hand
In six months a new one, for life

Med Adjustment

I would honestly think
Doubling up on a tranquilizer
Would have a far greater effect
Than it is having now
I don't feel any more tired
Which is a sign it's
Actually the correct medicine
And is helping relax me
Side effects, there aren't many
My mind is calmer
I forget a little more
But maybe that's just today
I'm sure it will take a while
To adjust to a new dosage
That has been fluctuating
For at least six years now
I've been somewhat dependant
Maybe a doctor's prescription
But a drug nonetheless

A Dream

Finally I remember a dream
But wishing I hadn't
I push it vigorously away
Like a lonely prisoner in a padded cell
Preoccupying myself works to an extent
And as always it resurfaces
The image of him losing his temper
Without a chance to respond
I'm awake wondering if it is a memory
Or just something I dreamt
Is it another sign
To get prepared for the worst
Without a bit of background detail
Just a quick idea floating by
I have no way of knowing
My sense of control is evaporating
When will I forget to catch my tongue
When will I pull the trigger

To the weapon aimed at me
And will it be slow or quick

Argument

I have no argument
With the term natural
But the following word:
Disasters, maybe not...
The earth is alive
We are made of it
It is not made of us
All intelligent organisms have anti-bodies
Hurricanes, Tornados, and Tsunamis
May be the defense mechanism
For a creature long tired
Of our persevering presence
Call them what you will
Maybe the planet's white blood cells
Relentlessly attacking the foreigners
Carelessly spreading their cancers
No matter really to us
The planet has the odds in its favor
No matter who wins the battle
Humans will one day be extinct

Living In

So many choices
When deciding how to live life
The past, present, or future
A combination, or just death
As a child others protect you
Steer you in what they think
Is the correct direction
And then the eighteenth birthday arrives
An adult able to die for their country
But still too young to have a beer
No need to get on that tangent

At eighteen most freedoms are realized
1. To live in the past
Is to dwell on what has happened
On things etched in stone
Things one has no control over
2. To live in the future
Is to gamble and be predictive
To make assumptions based on nothing
Putting faith in everything to work out
3. And my preference, to live in the present
To take each day and hour as it comes
Assume nothing and try to make the best of everything
Here a curve ball is no surprise, just a curve ball
4. Finally one can just give up
Decide life is not able to be "figured out"
That this puzzle of existence is too hard
And all the pieces will never fit together

Who's to Blame

Change is a given
Who is there to blame
And is there a point
In discovering the culprit
Some say that every action
Has an equal and opposite reaction
This may be true in scientific equations
But emotions are not so predictable
However one thing is always true
No situation or change designates a feeling
It is one's reaction to what happens
That determines the end result
One can train themselves to be numb
But then a new question arises
Can you be numb and still remain human
With all that happens in this world
Personally I tend to think no
There are no super-heroes that save the day
There are no fairy tale endings
Communication is the fabric that holds us

Choosing to bottle it all up
To hide it from all others
To vocalize your thoughts and feelings
Or be overwhelmed to various degrees
They are all part of being human
Learning continuously how regardless of its wonder
Life is and never will be fair
The only one left to blame is yourself

Untitled

This time isn't quite so bad
I can see the trees
And most of the forest
Clearly not as confused as before
Blaming myself seems a waste
Although my involvement is inevitable
I do not delegate these rules
Just decide what I feel is best for me
Having freed him from all his obligations
When this even occurs it will be his choice
Should I stay or should I go, up to him
And there will be no reprocussions either way
Yes I feel we are finally making progress
And my perks are all very nice
But these first few months with HER home
May be walking on eggshells, or easy
I honestly have no idea
I have never lived with a female
I don't fully understand what I am in for
And likely I won't until it happens
As for the other person I consider a friend
I'm helpless when it comes to assistance
As to what to say or do I'm clueless
And I fear there is no answer

Jealousy

I am amazed how quickly

Jealousy can set in
When one's life-long goal
Is to get attention
On a walk in circles
He sees her playing with her dog
Neither makes an approach
As I calmly observe
Her time appears used up
She leaves the gated field
And takes the easy way
Up the hill towards me
The dog is barking loudly
And she approaches and speaks
"My dog really dislikes strangers,
Could I have you throw the ball a few times"
Just a couple of tosses
And the interaction ended
She politely thanked me
And went on her merry way
His blood must have boiled
Gazing at me from below
Left curious and wondering
Why did she speak to me
When he was finished
He quickly jogged uphill
Demanding where I knew her from
I said only the truth
Her dog disliked me
So I threw it a ball
He remained unsatisfied

Traffic Jam

Four of the dreaded things
In less than twenty four hours
I made a plan of action
But the phone calls ended too quickly
Soon I decided to break a rule
I reached into the back seat
And retrieved funny looking cigarettes

Strawberry flavored and wrapped in a leaf
Trying to be discreet I lit one up
Several tries were needed with my lighter
Just a standard car push in device
Likely my fear of over-inhaling
For the first smoke in two to three years
I was smoking again
And the strawberry flavor
Was actually quite pleasant
For the nickel the smoke had cost
It seemed worth the risk
And as traffic began to move
I had a smile on my face
Fifteen minutes later, almost at my destination
I will still smoking the same cigarette
And my buzz must have been identical
To why people begin smoking the first time
Feeling dizzy and lightheaded
I threw the remains out a window
Trying to compose myself
And enjoy the warm feeling

A Move

After all these twenty seven years
In the same location and house
One of two bedrooms gets boring
And expectations for my apartment drop
Plain is just fine as far as I care
And the cheaper the better
No pets soon seems like a good idea
Who would watch them when I leave town
The two most important ingredients
For any place to work at this point
Are Anne and I agreeing it is okay
The rest becomes easy
In a matter of weeks
The place that has ALWAYS been home
Will become but a memory
And the "good life" can begin

No Common Sense

The smile plastered on my face
Along with the words on the page
Spelled out the truth of the situation
And how I had overlooked the obvious
As usual with a misunderstanding
I was totally open to hearing one side
Retorting occasionally, but being patient
So that I would truly understand
Too many incomplete thoughts
Being shared in a short span of time
Had created a built up anger
That was now diffused and disappeared
As I laughed at how stupid I had been
The offer was presented for me to yell
But I only smiled
Happy the friendship had not ended

Dropped Things

Throughout all my writings
And conversations about myself
The way I consider myself to be
And what does and does not work
I discovered my notions of me
Were not entirely correct
And that often when I calm down
I see there is nothing left to be angry about
It seems no matter how bad something appears
After the charged emotion subsides
I always can simply forgive and forget
Moving closer to the ideal me

Other Planes

When I think of all the things
A human eye is unequipped to see
It reminds me of how little of reality

We actually get to experience
If more parts of our brains worked
We might be seeing ghosts in graveyards
We could be seeing demons roaming the earth
And have so many more explanations
The voices "crazy" people hear
Might actually be audible to everyone
And that person has only unlocked
A new spectrum of existence

A Jump

Standing on the edge of my roof
Ground not too far down
Maybe four meters or less
That familiar feeling returned
A rush like the ones I had in childhood
How much would it hurt
If I just decided to jump
Or if I lost my balance

Not my fault

I sort of inadvertently
Figured out the problem
With few words exchanged
Only goal I had
Was to make sure
It was not me

Unfortunately for her
If I wasn't to know
It was a one or the other situation (or so I thought)
And if it isn't me
Process of elimination
Points to the culprit

We can't share our feelings
Because it will make things worse

So we both sit and wait
For the therapist appointment
Where we can spill our guts
And try to find an answer

Not my fault 2

What to do now
I was wrong again
More than two options were there
The problem remains
Not him or me
But I can't help but to care
It is a relief
And reduction of stress
That is wasn't right in front of my eyes
However no help
With the issue at hand
The cause and solution of cries
Answer: Butt Out!
Not your concern
Sometimes just better
To let some time pass
And stay completely out of the mix

Headache

My headache has stopped yelling
And is now only a whisper
Thanks to modern medicine
Or the placebo effect
I am curious why it hurts
If it is a physical reason
Built up stress or anxiety
Or just random pain
I would like a real target
To aim at when I shoot
Not just a vague idea
Like having a headache

My tolerance to these pills
Temporary fixes to a painful existence
Solve absolutely nothing
And get weaker by the day

A lady I know

She is a complete mystery
On days like today
Always angry at herself
If a few tears escape
Later on I might discover
A reason for the sadness
But for now I'll just assume
That it's my fault again
Something I said
Or something I did
That was too brutally honest
To not elicit these emotions
Got to improve on my charades
Need to learn to play nice
Occasionally try to be positive
Stop loading the dice
I just think it takes lots of time
When someone gets too close
And then turns and spits on you
To actually forgive them
I keep on going
But not for the right reason
Leaving myself confused
Everyone ends up getting bruised

A break

Finally a weekend like I remember them
Far from perfect, yet wonderful
Spending as much time as possible
Talking and touching the one I love
No graveyard nonsense to get me dirty

Less work than usual
Other things working themselves out
Even got along with my family (sister too!)
Then the realization hit me last night
I have three weeks of paperwork due
And only two days to finish
Over 120 pages from scratch
Today will be rushed like college
Procrastination once again not paying off
But I think it was worth it
Just to have a break from routine

Clover

In the past two days
I've spent a few minutes
A little here, a little there
In search of a four leaf clover
It seems like it would be a sign
Concrete evidence of good luck
Even if they are just mistakes
Mutations that occur randomly
There is likely no truth behind
Any clover bringing good luck
But I'll still continue to search
Who knows, I might get lucky

Weapons

Funny where my mind wandered
When I was upset last night
Remembering that broken bb pistol
That looked and felt so real
Actually considering
Use of complete terror tactics
To force the response I want
And ignore their wants completely
Again today when leaving home
I thought, what about a knife

Just something small for protection
In the case of an emergency
But no, I can't afford it
It will always be my fault
If anything happens
I would have to put on an act
That I was completely nuts
Sometimes disabilities seem unfair
And sometimes they are just handy excuses

Meeting

Exactly as I thought
Neither of us broke a smile
His forced apology
Got no forgiveness by me
No longer does he want
To attend church with me
What day should I pick
To suck up those hours
We exchanged one sentence
Between the two of us
And I assured his music
Was kept loud enough
We are both at the point
I often write about
Saying it could never happen
I never lose my temper
Well this is a test
I've already decided I won't
But when I get angry again
Will that decision hold true

Us

When will I learn
No matter how many times
I am advised to back down
To handle it professionally

I don't
I have to be held back
From what I know will be a mistake
My emotions take over
Just like his
Who really needs the help
From what I can figure now
Both of us

Nicknames

When we first met
You looked like violet
But if you were ever a blueberry
It would be very scary
I think it's funny Alison called you BFE
Cause I would make more fun about how you always have to pee
As far as you being Oscar
I think the real grouch gave me bloxter (a birthday present from my soon
to be father in law)
But when he calls you buggs
It's obvious he wants some hugs
If you were ever a real leezard
I would hunt down the evil wizard
With a nickname like bubbles
You probably caused lots of troubles
And now that you're a senior
It has changed your demeanor
I'll just call you AnnNuh
Cuz you love to eat bananas
And you know that you're the best
Now its time to take a rest

The Rain

It's no longer raining
And the brilliant bolts flashing overhead
Have moved to the next location
Leaving many clouds at sunset

I could kick myself at times like this
When the sky is so beautiful
And the hard wind keeps it ever changing
For having forgotten my camera
These are the images I dream of
Not only the colors of spring
But a trick and vibrant sky
Reflecting the last moments of daylight
Without these unnatural manmade markers
I could turn ninety degrees
And see something fully oppositional
To what I was just viewing
One could get lost in it
But humanity has made that impossible
Buildings, cars, roads, traffic, lights, people
They are all just in the way

Is it possible

Is it possible
To meet someone
And know them
Only a short time
Maybe just a day
But for them to have
Such a profound impact
Life as you know it stops
And something so much more beautiful
Replaces it for eternity
Can seconds with some
Overshadow years with others
Could one minute
Change everything
Are your friends
Better if they last longer
If you love them more
Or if they inspire you
To be the best you can
Time seems to have no relevance

Failing Memory

My memory is failing me is such a way
That a short cut ends up the long way around
I have no idea where I'm bound
Mile markers, road sings, and other frames of reference
Slowly become blurry as I drift along the street
Maybe only steps, just a few more feet
But not knowing where I'm going or where I've been
Leaves me clueless so I continue to walk
Wishing someone had the time to talk
Continuing I occasionally see chalk outlines
Curious and wondering if this was a joke
If not what were the last words they spoke
As I keep walking everything begins to fade
Eventually all the faces become one and the same
And they are just like me, I forgot my own name
Just another mindless zombie continuing
Trying to be unique and looking for a fix
To escape this never ending matrix

Paint

Every time I see you
You've removed some of the paint
The thick multiple layers
Of unbreathable skin you reside in
Sometimes it's entire layers
And others just a chip
But there is always change
Like an everlasting gobstopper
Only you have more guises
Than it has flavors
The rate at which you change
Much more gradual
I often wonder if you want help
But I suppose the shock
Of a nice paint thinner
Would overwhelm you

I'll always be curious
If and when you'll ever
Get back to the way you were
Before you needed protection

Untitled

I don't know what this is about
Maybe that's why it's such a scare
I can't tell if I should be happy or sad
All I know is it hits me there
Right in my heart and in my soul
Where the risk is ever more great
That no barriers will be thick enough
And it will permeate
Through my defenses so easily
Like a warm knife cutting butter
So worked up I am right now
I can't make sense of the clutter
All my levels rising up
Like a train whistle about to blow
Not only am I unsure what will help me
I have doubts even God would know
If so did would She help me along
Or am I walking all alone
Desperately needing a sign or signal
To decide to make itself known

Hypocrites

I think I would like church much more
If it weren't for all the hypocrites
Preaching about treating as you would like to be treated
But then about how other religions just aren't it
They have got it all mixed up
And do not understand
That we are right and they are wrong
That our God is "the man"
I don't recall the Bible calling

169

For us to engage in a holy war
She wants us all to get along
Destruction is not our chore
Talking about how all the Muslims
Will someday be judged by Her
Gives us no instruction or permission
To hate, persecute, and hunt them

Where is the gray

It's amazing how something as simple as keeping a promise
Following through with an agreement, being true to your word
Is usually much easier than going against it
But appears to be almost impossible to those who aren't honest
Blaming it on what you will, usually forgetfulness
It starts as a some time deal and develops into habit
Easier on your conscience to follow through with an agreement
Yet selfishness can overpower a person until they have no conscience
This leads to the ever unanswered question
Are all creatures innately born with the simple ability
To be able to see a black and white difference between good and bad
Or as time continues does the grey envelop us all
Being universally good or bad doesn't have a place in our world
Where each person, group, idea, and country disagree
There is no longer even a gray

Disaster called love

The inability to lie must be a bitch
It ruins one's chances at telling jokes
Never could you hold a poker face
Probably not even mask your feelings
Well they say opposites attract
Maybe that's why they ended up together
He could lie to his mother and bluff a bluffer
Visible emotion is foreign to him
Instead that plastered flat look with a smile
Not meant to portray sarcasm, contempt, or happiness
Just what others have always recommended

And a fake smile is so easy
But like us all he can't hold in laughter
When something is funny for any reason he understands
The tears almost begin to develop with giggling
She is much the other way, on this trait,
When angry no amount of any humor will help
Tickling, jokes, degrading oneself, movies, slapstick
She has the total control of her anger
The one thing they share is raising their voice
Although he much more guilty than she
Both have a need to strike a point and be heard
And somehow this disaster is what they call love

Less than…

Less than three weeks
Till I venture back into court
All payments secured
No more community service
Less than a miracle
I've made it thus far
Without breaking down
Or deciding to take chances
Less than 10 mph over
The posted speed limit
Or parking in the wrong place
No more bad Chreestopher
More than I'd hoped
The guilt eats me alive
Now sober to my deeds
Wrath and hate towards others
More than I'd seen
Eyes are now wide
To the motional damage
I continue to cause
More than I'd like
The hate in his eyes
On the point of a breakdown
And this is all my fault

Belt

I'm getting out my summer shorts
And now I always need a belt
They tend to just drop to the floor
Without a way to hold them up
The more I walk, the more I squirm
The more dangerous it gets
Without some sort of tightening buckle
They might as well be anklets
I fear the day when I forget
At the worst place and time
End up looking like an imbecile
Or someone committing a small crime
I am no streaker or voyeur
I just lost a little weight
But with so much going on
This just may be my fate

Surprise Party

Yesterday I helped to plan and carry out
A surprise birthday party for someone
But I had to keep in mind one thing
I refused to tell lies to help it happen
The difficulty wasn't impossible
My fondness of bending the truth
And moving in slow motion
Helping it to all come together
The surprise was a success
And much better than I expected
Decorations, Pizza, Cake, presents
With my camera to catch it all
Unfortunately I forget an important detail
Candy and snacks should not be presents!
I told no one, and they all helped
To overdo the party with food
The agreement we made with food
Was shattered overnight
So we got out the scale

How did the weight go away?

Community Service 2

Still nothing really beats
Getting paid for nothing
And although I'm not being
Paid
I am being credited for sitting
While others dig a grave
Listening to a few songs
Writing in my book of words
Just waiting for my turn
After today I will have 60%
Of my total time complete
More than halfway on my quest
To return to normal life
Where Saturdays do not start
At seven thirty am
In a place of resting souls
For some cleanup duty

Last Day

Today is it
No coming back
Don't have to watch
The demeaning behavior
They live together
But her patience
Wears so thin
That yelling is the only response
I bet if I lived
Without someone like her
I would have to have quiet hour
Or maybe quiet day…or life

Wondering

He stands on the pool exercising
Not knowing the exact words
But from his face I can tell
He knows it's about him
When will he figure it out?
These pages are more than poems
They are non-audible communications
To his mother
If he ever learns to read
These pages would incriminate me
Do I really want to take the chance?
Of them being discovered
It's an oxymoron
The harder I work to help him read
The more likely he will some day
Be able to read this
Although reading and understanding are different
Even catching the gist
Of these hateful words
Would be a bomb exploding

Computer

I am so cocky
Mr. fix it
Well this time
I was clueless
Even reading instructions
And guided by professionals
My computer has issues
That I don't enjoy
Still the chance
To erase it all
Start from scratch
And hope it works
Either way I chose
I'm left with a final solution
Pay someone with more experience

To diagnose and fix my problem
Funny this is
The problems are nothing
Minor annoyances
That disrupt what I considered perfection

Meds

It's very interesting
I can feel physical effects
Of my required tranquilizers
But mentally, nothing
Maybe I did it again
Decided that it would not work
And my will power is so strong
That it isn't working at all
However unlikely that seems
It could be true
Or even worse it is working
And I'm just that mad
Just like last time
And every time before that
After my weekend
Things will be fine
We can both pretend
Nothing happened and we're friends
Until we achieve full circle
And start over again

I don't get it

I don't understand
His unhealthy obsession
With comparing himself to others
And pushing on the boundaries
One simple fact I know
No two people are alike
Not even siblings have the same circumstances
All comparisons are useless

Testing something for stability
Can be a healthy behavior
But jumping on something fragile
Will eventually make it break
Does it really matter?
If the rules are different
For different people
I would argue no
The world is an unfair place
And two people are unfairly matched
What is normal for one person?
May be deadly for another

Strengths and Weaknesses

To me some things were always natural
But to those around me they seem foreign
Almost as if the ideas never occurred to them
Yet it could be such a helpful tool
Parents want one thing and boy wants another
Sometimes he decided to do it his way
Then comes the problem and dilemma
That I don't fully grasp
If a parent threatens with a light punishment
I would, in his shoes, make that seem terrible
Promises not to make the mistake again
Put on an act that I am very sad
The situation becomes a win/win
Punishment that is so bad
You make parents feel bad too
Both groups have in essence gotten their way
Boy does not follow my example
Repeats he doesn't care, it doesn't matter, and it won't help
Reactions repeatedly get more rational
Yet still he remains emotionless and angry
And leaves room for only last resorts
The situations becomes a lose/lose
Punishment is far too harsh
Parents think child is impossible and begin to give up
Child is left with nothing

I hate to be teaching how to lie
But it could prove to be useful
When used appropriately in situations
Where boy just hurts himself
Longing to be treated as an adult
But all actions that of a child
Stuck in a limbo

Hidden

I've been hiding
So I won't get hurt
Behind an invisible barrier
That only exists for me
When anyone gets too close
I decide on a course of action
A comment or an action
Intended to push away
Throwing them off track
Making them rethink things
When nothing has changed
I'm still who I am
I've become so good at it
It is second nature
It's a reflex
And has taken over
Now rather than be
The person buried under the camouflage
I react as if programmed
Into a complex computer

Focused

Unable to stay focused
For even five minutes
Something unaware to the world
He sees or hears it
What these hallucinations, voices, demons are
Isn't important

But how to make them go away
Is approaching the top of the list
Feeling each day
More determined and able
To solve this galactic mystery
Of what makes a person tick
How long will it be?
Until the next unexpected behavior emerges
Drowning out all the reality
Leaving itself in control

Some things make him appreciate life

Some things make him really appreciate life
While at the same time sending his mind in circles
Spinning wildly, yet still under control
Perhaps the explanation for all the medication
For days like this, so he couldn't be overcome
But this story of a friend needs to be told
He needs to share his feelings aloud
But law prohibits some of his actions
Bottled up it reminds him of his father
Soon the body to be forever encaged in a box
And the struggle for the soul, if there is one
And then what will happen to it
Well versed in blaming others or himself
He decides to blame no one
A tragedy is still a tragedy without reasons
But his heart hangs low today

Church Camp

Yeah all those memories can be nice
The people who were so sweet
The jokes we played on one another
But one memory reached the surface yesterday
The day a friend from my youth group
Found it necessary to punch my face
Surprised I did not react at all

The others crowded him and held him back
HA!, holding HIM back, what a joke
His neck like a brittle twig
If I released the anger at that point
There would remain a room of motionless bodies
I instead remained still until those words emerged
Threats, bad language, an explosion of sound
But I calmed down and just walked away
Never to forgive him

Maybe it's time

<u>What a life...</u>

It's unfair that he can just turn it off
Even though he's been training
Going from angry enough to destroy
To docile as a snail in minutes
The trainer obviously does not practice what he preaches
Starting the day off on the wrong foot
Feeling it continue forever
And only the quiet will help him relax
He has no picture of happiness
No ever-present bed to relax on
No right to pull out a radio and ignore the world
Work is what it is he must just behave
While the other cool as a cucumber
Doesn't give his mentor the break he needs
Starts right in on a conversation
As if nothing has gone wrong at all
After being told the quiet is okay
He says yesterday he needs sleep
And without thinking he gets a reply
"You only stayed asleep for 20 min"
Immediately a reply "R U trying to start an argument?"
As quick "NO!" and "lets just be quiet" (like he said to begin with)
Then a silent drive to the destination
But regardless of the next 3 hours
Mr. mentor is still boiling inside

Naked

He lay naked on the floor
Uncovered and without embarrassment
Embracing himself as whole
And unconcerned with others
Suddenly it began to make sense
Why the friendships had dwindled
Upon realizing he was complete
He needed no gaps to be filled
Before when he tried to 'fix' people
He thought it was the reason for companionship
Now realizing how wrong he was
He began to smile and laugh at his foolishness

Scared

He spent a while thinking
Contemplating what he could not handle
What his own definition of fear was
And decided he could handle it alone
Nothing could ever be so powerful
That another emotion could not compensate
Never would he be so scared
That anger could not cure it

What am I talking about?

He realizes it makes him shallow
To have such impure thoughts
Yet thinks it better to be honest
Than lie about what he considers obvious
Upon a first impression he notices one thing first
Next the eyes, facial features, clothing style, hair
Color of hair not important, ethnicity not important
Religion not important, Body size not important
Obviously this is the first impression
Before words are spoken

Once they are a voice can be intoxicating
And meeting the real person overtakes all
Personality goes a long way is an understatement
It almost totally decides where the relationship will go
Friends, acquaintances, lovers, nothing, soul mates
Never once considering-what will his family think
He doesn't care because beauty is only skin deep
Even the one thing he first notices
Can and will likely change like everything else
But qualities not visible to the eye
Are much harder to change
And tend to last closer to a lifetime
Than the superficial beauty
That jogs through his head

Complete Me

I've been wandering around for ages
Looking for that perfect person
The one who could complete me
The one to fix all the wounds others have caused

Now I'm getting married in two months
But I have finally figured it all out
No one can complete me but me
No one can heal me but myself

And as I become more complete
So does my life and everyone around me
Things begin to blossom where there was nothing
And I am begging to see the biggest part of me is me

Not to downplay my fiancée's role
She keeps me sane
With the help of lots of medication
And lots of friends that love me dearly

But they can't fix or heal me
It's up to me to make the decision for myself
And to actually follow through with it

Which is what I have been doing

I had no time for pity writing
Because I have been becoming myself
For the first time in my life
I am just letting go and being me

I feel like I could do just about anything
But I realize what I am doing is perfect
Everyday is just another adventure
And each breath is something to be thankful for

Opposites attract?

This myth I don't consider true
A perfect opposite of you
Would have opinions and thoughts
That created a magnet
Can you imagine your most ambitious dream
Being someone's absolute worst nightmare
And actually thinking this was the one
The courtship would have to be quick
The initial heart flutters and crush
Could not have worn off long enough
To actually have a discussion
It would probably have to be all physical
This myth also discounts any homosexual couple
There are not true opposites like male and female
The two would never actually agree on anything
But one would be dominant and one submissive
One would compliment the other's strengths
Because they would be their weaknesses
Yet again if one is nice then the other is mean
And most mean people don't hand out compliments
The simple truth is some people just click
It's not about similarities, differences, looks, beliefs
Its more about what you can't see and is hard to describe
There is and never will be a formula for love

Heart in my hand

He used to believe
There was only one way to love
With his heart in his hand
So she could know the real him
After many attempts
More than he could remember
He began to shut down
Almost no heart remained
Emotions seemed foreign
Except for anger
Which was always underlying
Even every smile
The heart had been picked at
Torn up, and devoured
leaving only a hard seed
Then his mind forced a change
And he began hiding his seed
Nourishing himself and not others
Some would say he was self-centered
Soon enough the seed sprouted and began to grow
It got back to it's original size
But had potential to get much bigger
using a fertilizer he did not have
So the search began again
To find that magical person
Who could make his heart grow
And in return he could do so for her

Last thing you said

Those last few words
The phrase before goodbye
Kept ringing in his ear
For what seemed like an eternity
Funny how short term memory
Doesn't always work correctly
but occasionally something sticks
And may last forever

183

These particular last three words
Reminded him of a truth
He would never tire of hearing
Always warming him up inside
The best part was soon
On the next phone call
Or the next time at home
It wasn't just a faint ring
She was saying it again
Because it is the truth

Innocence

At what point does a person
Cross the threshold from which
One cannot return back to the beginning
And once again be innocent
Is there such a point
Or perhaps never too late
For an old dog to learn new tricks
And a person to reclaim their life
Dropping all the bad habits and behaviors
Returning back to square one
Unable to change one's ago
But to start again with all one knows
Everyone says if I knew then what I know now
Isn't it enough to just know it now
It's never too late to make a change
And today is a great day to start

From here

Directions had been left
And he had followed them till now
Although occasionally confusing
There was somewhat of a path
But no longer did a voice speak
The map he carried turned to dust
And without a destination given

Left to figure it out
The thought reoccurring in his head
Like a beating drum
Where to go from here
The tempo gradually increasing
Then all at once it stopped
And as he reopened his eyes
The answer became clear as crystal
He was already there

Cry all you want

He doesn't care
Maybe it's the easy way
But as much as she cries
He will not work it out
The chances given
To start over
Much too numerous
The pity was shown long ago
Giving in at this point
Would only show weakness
And he must make sure
To not be taken advantage of
The 20/20 retrospect
Always as clean as a glass pane
He realizes this had been coming
For quite some while
Always told not to burn bridges
But she has burned him
Disfigured his heart
And revenge is becoming prevalent
He walks away
Leaving her unsheltered in the rain
Coming from an emotional storm
She brought on herself

Another Bedroom

He hates himself for what he cannot do
He hates himself for what he put her through
He hates himself for thinking that he really grew
Into someone brighter than this old and dingy blue

She cries all night wondering what he is thinking
She cries all night pondering the thought of drinking
She cries all night to keep herself from sinking
Into the depths much deeper than visible when blinking

From a door away he hears her pacing down the stairs
From a door away he knows right now that she has no cares
From a door away he remembers all that's caused the tears
Into both hearts so deeply that there's likely no repairs

She wonders if he loves her and if he's going to stay
She wonders if he'll cling to her or if he'll betray
She wonders if those drugs he did are just waiting at bay
For the chance to suck him back into a total disarray

Talking never solves anything because they are stubborn
Talking is a last resort, like sunscreen after sunburn
Talking not and damage done, but alone it can sit and churn
Into a disaster worse than death, such a sad way to learn

Tonight they begin sleep without the comfort of someone else's heat
Then she knocks and begs for him to come to bed to meet
Sleeping in the hall way, a last resort to be at his feet
So when he rises he will see that this is for life, not just a heartbeat

A Desert of Memories

It would be nice
If I could take back what I said
Although I get forgiveness
Nothing is forgotten
Every action one takes
Leaves footprints in a sand
Where the wind never blows
And the tracks become concrete

Luckily most choose not
To dwell in this desert
Of memories and past
But pay it no mind

Why?

Sometimes I sit pondering
Why things are as they are
Usually it has nothing to do with me
But I'm often blind to the fact
Maybe I should not try
To find meaning in everything
Analyzing beneath the surface
Missing obvious beauty
Sometimes yes just means yes
And no just means no
Requiring a reason
Just a waste of time

Road Sign

Who made this sign
Thirteen miles per hour
Why not ten or fifteen
Twelve and a half would be middle
Rounding up perhaps
But to an "unlucky" number
Doesn't seem likely
It's a coincidence
Maybe someone like me
Out for a little fun
Laughing each time
They see their sign

Man's Best Friend

Dogs not for me
How can dogs be so stupid
As to wag tails while barking
Can't they make up their minds
Do they have emotions and souls
Or is it just a long list of tricks
Conditioned to respond a certain way
No smarter than a mouse
Sniffing out cheese in a maze
I prefer cats
No mistaking of intention
Not only do they clean themselves
They are independent
Purr when happy, hiss when angry
Refuse to learn tricks, unless by their choice
More instinct than conditioning
More natural than humanized
Complete with a unique soul

Man Holes

I used to think
Drain pipes lead to tunnels
Wondrous underground communities
They must have them somewhere
To force such strange ideas in my head
Or just television
Like Ninja Turtles and IT's monster clown
Planting ideas
I used to think
Friends almost grew on trees
Easy to find and keep forever
Until I was betrayed
In a cycle that made me more careful
Which deserved that title
From the list of users and abusers
That fill my life
I used to think
True love an illusion
Impossible a match made just for me

Complimenting my strengths
Understanding each of my weaknesses
To share my smiles and tears
In a relationship defeating time
But I was wrong

For A #2

If I knew then
What I know now
I would try to keep things the same
And not correct each blunder
Although many mistakes I've made
Each led me to the present
And maybe a slight change
Would ruin my newfound bliss
Though I can't predict the future
I can believe in...
The power of love
There are no coincidences
God has a plan for me
Things will work out as they should
and promises can last a lifetime
Knowing all this
my petty regrets miniaturize
Because the most important thing
Is the look in her eyes

Topic for Discussion

Is one valid argument
To believe in one but not the other
When one thinks it through
Maybe so
Before the seven days began
There were angels and God
And angels were as powerful to Her
As an ant is to an elephant
Then man was created in Her image

And we became Her most prized creation
Above all others, including the angels
Some, rightfully so, were enraged
For an angel to man
Is also like an elephant to an ant
No matter how large the army
The elephant can and will prevail
But some of the angels created an uprising
And their army was crushed
They were banished forever
To a torturous world
Absent of the one ingredient they needed, God
He gave us free will
The ability to know right from wrong
A book to guide us on the path
And a way to get into heaven
One is left wondering
Where is the devil in all this
A fallen angel sentenced to rot for eternity in hell
What power has that over us
Absolutely none, we make our mistakes alone
And with the knowledge of their consequences

At it again

Finally he forced himself to believe
It really has nothing to do with him
Only an issue better dealt with alone
Than with his or anyone's company
Still wishing he had the words
A potion to cure her pain
A way to begin to understand
What it is that bothers her
But a little voice in his head
Repeats the phrase until he moves on
If she could tell you, she still would't
And he realizes that is the only way

Peace is...

Peace is hard
Even for just one person
To not be over-critical
Of all the faults you see
In others but not yourself
Point of view error

Sometimes to get along
With other people without incident
You have to be like a limb in the wind
Willing to bend to the point of breaking
Not showing even a tiny sign
Of stress, exhaustion, or limits

Many religious people think
Only God can bring you peace
That it is unachievable by us
That God must lead us there
In this life or the next
And we are but pawns

But if granted free will
Then God only intervenes
When we ask for the right reasons
And since no one knows
What those reasons are
The set of footprints are likely ours

God is perfect-so She can fly
No need for Her to make footprints
Who says She even has feet
Peace is a state of mind
Paying attention to each thought
And behaving appropriately without help

Nice Chatting

Today he got the chance
He's been waiting for

Able to make a comment
That actually started conversation
So rare the opportunity presents itself
Without having to reach at all
That he took hold
And with just a smile it began
Both agreed what is life
Without an occasional difference
Maybe the exact words she used were
A mediation from the norm
During a simple exercise class
She decided to be wild and do her own thing
Laughing, Jumping, Twisting, Turning
Just having a good time for her
After their talk he relaxed
And just thought how great it really is
To break away from the routine
And do something nice just for yourself

First compulsive act

Since the new medication
He has had no compulsive acts
Well maybe just a few
But spending money was under control
Then came yesterday
Away from home and on the computer
Seeing something he did not need
But would possibly be helpful in one way
The purchase was made
Over twenty five dollars on cards
He had ceased to play ten years ago
Until the last month
Finally with a new opponent
One he never loses to
unless he is being merciful
He buys more cards on a whim
Just to be more effective
In absolute decimation

Combining treasures from all around
For his own immediate gratification

Monkey

Oh God, what should I do
For a moment, maybe an hour
There is no monkey to amuse him
There is no immediate gratification
Out of character for his age, but not him
He continuously returns to look at that
Which he no longer can afford
A silly game that he cannot finish
Pumping quarters repeatedly into a slot
Doing what he is here for
And then returning to the addiction
Bright lights and a steering wheel
When the quarters run out
There will be only one question
Will he ask to "borrow" money
That he never intends to repay

Still Going

Back at this familiar but uncomfortable place
Where it's very likely that my feelings will be hurt
When each day can be full of ups and downs
And I cannot prepare for or expect anything
Yes the weekend is over
Sad to see life in these bleak terms
But I've survived damn near everything
And that keeps me going most of the time

Unnatural

A "normal" person caught in a lie
Comes up with excuses
Tries to reason and bargain

If nothing else somehow denies it
But we are not all socialized creatures
Whether right or wrong, some care not
Maybe not even purposeful or lethargic
They have never learned this behavior
In my life I am attempting
To stop taking things as constants
And in that quest I feel this one person
May aid me more than an army could
Never knowing what to expert
How or why behaviors emerge
Just that they are present
And must be neither ignored
Not trigger my automatic response
That's been programmed into me forever
To behave the proper way
I must also un-socialize myself
It's aggravating

Curve Ball

In the new quest I've begun
In order to evolve into a better person
I'm finding it difficult not to speak
When an obvious lie is being stated
Remembering that this test
My way of viewing my own existence
Requires many different ideas
And maybe nothing can be taken for granted
I decided to shut my mouth and go outside
With the random ideas to clean out my car
Somewhat of a curveball to my usual hovering
Following and demanding the leadership role I've stepped into
And just as I predicted, almost immediately the words erupt
"Where have you been?," almost as if I'm babysitting
Explaining quickly I sit down and begin writing
Just staying to myself and relaxing
This complete jigsaw and wondrous creature
Who changes multiple times a second

Is sometimes as predictable as a goldfish
When their security is threatened

Surprisingly Well

Today is going surprisingly well
Somehow in just a few days
I have made leaps and bounds
In my quest to understand them
Asked to smile and laugh more
I created a true/false list
Of interesting life events for me
That I thought might bring smiles
Lo and behold it worked
And for a minutae moment
We both shared a bond
Greater than any chain
And they began to open up
Later they insulted my poetry
Referring to it as scribble I believe
And lied about our game stats
So I happy agreed
Maybe for them admitting defeat
Is only a loss for them
But not a win for me
Who cares, I kept my mouth shut!
I let the words roll off my back
I made fun of myself to create laughter
Where before silence had filled the room
The actual statements being made
Between the two of us are becoming less important
And the actual intent
Is beginning to shine through

Pieces Don't fit

The pieces of this dark puzzle
Do not fit together
The hypocrisy boils over them

Every statement is an oxymoron
But they are so far from a moron
As Mr. Gump was from being a genius
Yes Forrest understood some simple ideas
That they have forgotten along the ride
In their shoes I can't imagine
Being ordinary, with manners and friends
Waking up one day with unimaginable fear
having the walls of your world tumble inward
And all sight of friend or acquaintance disappear
Ending up hearing multiple voices
But not all in your head
Actually surrounding you in a hospital
Where everyone but you appears insane
In AA they say acceptance is the first step
But how to accept something you feel is real
Is only a fabricated extension of yourself
Manifesting audibly and visually to you
Is actually just your mind
Playing dirty tricks on you
Like realizing you're in a dream
But not being able to awaken

Someone Different

Unable to stay focused
For even five minutes
Something unaware to the world
They see or hear it
What these hallucinations, voices, demons are
Isn't important
But how to make them go away
Is approaching the top of the list
Feeling each day
More determined and able
To solve this galactic mystery
Of what makes a person tick
How long will it be
Until the next unexpected behavior emerges

Drawing out all of reality
Leaving itself in control

The process

He was a boy scout
He understood knots
He could make a Noose
But never had a reason
Jim had a reason
He clumsily made a Noose
And with no knowledge
About ropes or regard for himself
Imagining how it was done
Brought shudders down his spine
Without the proper tools
A knot was very slow
No pop, or even a broken neck
No instantaneous death
More like an ever so slow strangulation
Gasping for breath till the end
Why Jim's life seemed so good
To all those who cared
He would never know
But forever contemplate

Why not the lie?

Why couldn't the lie be true
Rather his sister than his friend
She doesn't deserve a tenth chance
It's been too long since a consequence
Much easier it would have been
Because I think she doesn't matter
Then again my family would be torn
With me left as the comforter
This is just a lose situation
Nothing good comes from suicide
The coward's easy way out

Hurts those around him all the more
Never to see another sunrise
Never to see another first snow
Unable to watch his puppet grow up
And his birth mother may never know

Unplugged

As he listens to the words
Without all the noise
He believes more and more
Today's poets are song writers
Their meaning takes on so much more
Without the drums, static, changes
Those occur in a studio
With just clear words
All those times he sung it wrong
For so many songs
Or just hummed
Begin to make sense
And he knows
One great way to feel good
Is to just lie back
Into a pillow of singing voices

Oops

He forgot one important thing
Before grabbing his lunch bag
Walking to the car
And heading to work
As soon as traffic was entered
The realization came to him
By not having breakfast
He'd forgotten all the pills
Vitamins for good health
Happy pills for mood
Relax pills for excitement
Rationality pills for spending

Now the test beings
Is it all just in his head
With an un-precedented placebo effect
Or is he crazy?
Unwilling to take the chance or test
He makes a memorable illegal U-turn
Reopens the front door
And decides he can be late for once

Three years

Three years to the day
And here we both stay
Locking in at each glance
So strong our romance
The friends that were there
Now we both share
And each family
Is becoming one tree
In months less than three
Then there will be
A joining in matrimony
To last for eternity

I wish I could say it's over

Although today could not have been better
My fear and anxiety were pushed aside
In just a few moments after arriving
One point was made clear
My disclaimer is not enough
The fact that I only use approved names isn't enough
I must actually edit my thoughts
No longer can I use the internet
As such a simple solution to what ails me
I have to fall back to the computer
And when calm, re-read and edit
That is not an issue of fair or unfair
It's also not an issue of my rights

It basically boils down to one simple idea
Am I stupid enough to keep asking for punishment
The answer is no
Maybe I should cease to use the word "I"
After all "I" don't want anyone to know me
"I" want to be a mystery

Life up to Now pt 1

His whole life had been
A series of ups and downs
never too high or low
Likely close to normal
Then age 16 hit
When the big secret
Someone he loved had been hiding
Came out
Devastation was the only description
Then the medications began
Yes, he was suicidal
But not strong enough to follow through
Depression stayed until college
Where he took the self-medicating route
Slowing moving closer and closer to
That "normal" he had as a child
Throughout this process he was like a caterpillar
Going into a cocoon
And slowing becoming a butterfly
that avoided danger only by a hair
the transformation from boy to man
From timid and bashful to strong and forward
Totally introverted to a bit extraverted
From a goodie two shoes to a rebel
After college all the statements he had always been told rang true
His degree was not enough to make real money
People he loved always ended up leaving him
Life was very far from a fairy tale

Part 2-the Plateau

In the midst of bad relationships
Poor decisions, and compulsive spending
He met her and things started to improve
Maybe most important, the drugs stopped
Soon he became more picky about friends
And eager to get back in touch
With all those high school buddies
He had left back before college
He began to have doctors and counselors
Experiment to find out what medications
Would be helpful to him the most
There was plenty of trial and error
He found a good job, paying what they said it couldn't
And it was wonderful work, lots of fun
And after two years with his girlfriend he proposed
And then had a fiancée
It seemed the fairytale might happen
As this streak of never-ending good took over
Getting along with his family like never before
Next he got his own place to live
Medication changes a little bit, some up, some down
And immediately the anxiety from yesterday hit
He is at a plateau, a high dive, a skyscraper
So high he could not survive a slip or fall
And he thinks about the past...
How up until now it never worked out
The anxiety starts to set in
It has to happen, but when?...

Scam

Fell for it again
Win this for free
Just fill out a survey
And agree to some offers
Well I got nothing for free
But I agreed to so many
Offers I will never use
To work toward my prize

How could I be so stupid
I need a new browser
One that removes ads
From all windows always
The temptation of such
A great reward
Cost me plenty in shipping
For crap I don't need
That bit of change
Could have been
The first amount set aside
Towards buying my reward
Why do I get a reward
For proving to myself once again
That I don't have to buy compulsively
I can save up money gradually

My Way

Finally writing again
And with good reason
The medication regime has changed
And some of the feelings have resurfaced
Regardless of their nature
It feels wonderful
To have a bit of spectrum
Past contact, manic, or angry manic
Doing more laughing and smiling
Finally those endorphins that have been
Building for over a year easily
Can be released as needed
The small things are a big deal
They always have been
But usually only the small annoyances
Not the small pleasures
Following the Dr's exact orders
Re-reading them twice to be sure
I want to experience the withdrawal
That comes with a quick taper instead of gradual
Yes, someone today said I look tense

More so than they have ever seen
But I enjoy being intense
I don't want life to get boring

Good nights Sleep

Maybe he's reaching
For heights unachievable
But tonight for the first time
In thirteen long years
Half his entire lifetime
The bed he sleeps in
Will actually be long enough
So many possibilities
Stretch out, no curling up
Enjoy the feel of the new
Expensive posture perfect mattress
Maybe even dreams will be remembered
Because REM sleep will occur more frequently
On a sleeping surface
That is made to hold him
Looking forward to sleep
like never before
First time his money
Has been involved at all
When it comes to 4AM tomorrow
He intends to be asleep
No waking up
Maybe sleeping through the alarm

Rumors

When he hears something
About someone else
He goes straight to the source
Rather than believing anyone
Trustworthy or not
No point in knowing
Unless the person involved

Wanted him to know
We need to stop all these
Rumors that populate our words
Growing with each silly person
Unable to trace it to the beginning
Pick up a phone
Call a person
Get the answer they want you to have
And there it ends
Not to be repeated
Or explained to those
Who perpetuated the lie
Let them learn on their own

Per Request

I had begun to think
No one cared about participation
Just a simple head count
But then I was asked
To be a working piece
Of a moving unit of people
Instead of just watching from
The sidelines where I phase out
Admitting afterwards to myself
Much more rewarding inside
Than just a silent representation
Of a voiceless population

Predictions

Beginning to think I'm in the wrong profession
Doing such an excellent job predicting events
Most are soap opera and not real life
But still, I have no access to the scripts
Maybe I could have been a psychic
Adding up the context clues to a situation
Coming up with the likely outcomes
And giving each a percentage based weight

I know, it sound stupid for a career
But as a fall-back I could always write for a soap
I think I could add a lot of humor
And a heck of a lot more unpredictability
Also I could be a good enough writer
To extinguish the need for all this filler
Pointless repetition and lines that don't deserve
To ever be allowed in a script
Days could be accomplished once an hour
So ridiculous jumps from season to season
And time warps for holiday specials would disappear
And more stories could happen than one
Of course, I only watch one soap opera
But at a glace the other day at another
A baby's thoughts were coming to fruition in a bubble
How stupid Americans must seem to foreigners

Too many chances

Listen to yourself
You sound just like
Those other people
You used to give advice
What good was it
If you don't follow it yourself
These people are getting way
Too many chances to make it
Occasionally a second chance
Depending on the seriousness
Of the mistake or crime
Can be in order
But for those who
Can't handle forgiveness
Teach them the hard way
Show absolutely no remorse
You are only helping
Make them continue this cycle
Of abuse and lies
To everyone they know
Be a hero

Stand up for what is right
A leader and not a follower
One cheek is always enough

Finally

Her tears have stopped
Maybe temporarily
But everyone needs a break
As long as it's not forever
I would not wish this curse
Of always appearing serious
Or completely loopy
On anyone
Life without tears
Is not much of a life
But too many
Is also a waste
If one turns up like me
Having used them all up
On book reports and nervous situations
It feels odd to be fine at a funeral
Imagine hearing the most important person
In the world to you being brutally murdered
And not one tear can fall
Appearing to be ambivalent
Let me tell you from experience
Not that anyone I know was murdered
But plenty of people have died
And I always look the same
Some applaud my strength
If they could only see the inner turmoil
That is only multiplied
By the lack of tears

Electronic Drain

My pocket sized entertainment unit
No, not something sexual, my game boy
Finally ran out of power

Boy did it ever keep going
Now August, last charged in March
Played countless times, especially recently
Probably 25 hours in the last three weeks
And now just two hours fixes it
In this field, where sometimes I sit
Hour upon hour just watching
This little bit of technology
Has kept me sane, but probably aided to headaches
Maybe today I won't have one
Who knows what lies ahead
But I needn't worry
Tomorrow has no game time

MY SPACE

That is the perfect name
Meaning a space for me
Looking as I wish it to look
Visible by only those approved
Finally I can do mass communications
Without a form letter
And ever better yet
I'm not telling anyone
No letter is arriving
Saying, "hey, I sent you a letter"
They must come on their own
To see what's going on
Meaning those that read
Actually care
It means so much more
Than a stupid counter reading +1
Where before I goofed
I feel now secure and safe
I can say what I want to
Without the usual fear
That some random statement
However innocent it may appear to me
Is going to be read incorrectly
And start all the trouble again

Serious

Been a while since I've been asked
"Why are you so serious"
Man, I hate that question
I usually can't come up with an answer
And on this occasion there is one
It's never nice so I don't use it
Today I guess several things
Are making me less comical than usual
I chose to blame it on sleepiness
But I really don't believe that
He is utterly silent
Not a work
Just driving with music
Paying me no attention
Then the question...
Well, I was reading about my friend today
The one who now is dead
And it made me sad
Truth, yes, but it doesn't work
So I sort of change the subject
If being serious criteria is just quiet
I could ask him plenty about being serious
But I don't
That would be unfair
And honestly I don't know
Thinking of answers just brings more questions
Perhaps the solution
Is to put it back on him
"Give me a reason to smile"
Never know till you try

Why no Super-Heroes?

There are no super-heroes
For many reasons
Of course they are imaginary
And humans just aren't made that way
But more importantly
People with power exploit it
They don't use it to help their neighbor
But to take control
Also a super-hero's job
Is to help other people
And in this world we live in
They all want to do it themselves
There is no way to force it
And it's very unlikely a super-hero
Could even help themselves
Look at it like this
To love someone else, first love yourself
To help someone else, first help yourself
And our problems never end

At Bay

Holding the feelings at bay
He can only do it so long
It is not a solution
Just a temporary fix
Under the feelings
That with time
This gash will heal itself
And tears wont be needed
Underneath he knows
He is just playing a game with himself
Unable to win or lose
Just postpone the inevitable
Maybe perhaps work out one problem
At a time instead of tackling the mound
He has let form while pretending
Perfection is easily achieved

The next day

Not everything is perfect
But that lucky shirt
Had an important impact
On my life yesterday
The big picture
For the rest of the world
Hasn't changed at all
Not even a bit of color
But I got my job back
My finger hurts less
And all the good things
Are still in place

Obsession

I don't understand
His unhealthy obsession
With comparing himself to others
And pushing on the boundaries
One simple fact I know
No two people are alike
Not even siblings have the same circumstances
All comparisons are useless
Testing something for stability
Can be a healthy behavior
But jumping on something fragile
Will eventually make it break
Does it really matter?
If the rules are different
For different people
I would argue no
The world is an unfair place
And two people are unfairly matched
What is normal for one person?
May be deadly for another

So terrible

I have no argument
With the term natural
But the following word:
Disasters, maybe not…
The earth is alive
We are made of it
It is not made of us
All intelligent organisms have anti-bodies
Hurricanes, Tornados, and Tsunamis
May be the defense mechanism
For a creature long tired
Of our persevering presence
Call them that you will
Maybe the plants' white blood cells
Relentlessly attacking the foreigners
Carelessly spreading either cancers
No matter really to us
The planet has the odds in its favor
No matter who wins the battle?
Humans will one day be extinct

Bolts

It is no longer raining bolts
And the brilliant flashing overhead
Has moved to the next location
Leaving many clouds at sunset
I could kick myself at times like this
When the sky is so beautiful
And the hard wind keeps it ever-changing
For having forgotten my camera
These are the images I dream of
Not only the colors of spring
But a thick and vibrant sky
Reflecting the last moments of daylight
Without these unnatural manmade markers
I could turn ninety degrees

And see something fully oppositional
To what I was just viewing
One could get lost in it
But humanity has made that impossible
Buildings, cars, roads, traffic, lights, people
They are all just in the way

Hidden

I've been hiding
So I won't get hurt
Behind an invisible barrier
That only exist for me
When anyone gets too close
I decide on a course of action
A comment or an action
Intended to push away
Throwing them off track
Making them rethink things
When nothing has changed
I'm still who I am
I've become so good at it
It is second nature
It's a reflex
And has taken over
Now rather than be
The person buried under the camouflage
I react as if programmed
Into a complex computer

Focused

Unable to stay focused
For even five minutes
Something unaware to the world
He sees or hears it
What these hallucinations, voices, demons are
Isn't important
But how to make them go away

Is approaching the top of the list
Feeling each day
More determined and able
To solve this galactic mystery
Of what makes a person tick
How long will it be?
Until the next unexpected behavior emerges
Drowning out all the reality
Leaving itself in control

Still Feeling

Still feeling half asleep
I make an obvious effort
To make it though another day
The stress is overwhelming
In an attempt to relax yesterday
I took a few benadryl for sleep
But of course I slept wrong
On my back creating neck pain
Now I am not only tired and cranky
But my neck has a reduced range of motion
In such a hurry last night
I did not wash my bathing suit
The hot tub could work wonders
Towards loosening me up
And relieving this awful pain
That I can't get used to

Asleep

My mind is still asleep
But I am physically awake
Somewhere between dreams and life
How did I make this mistake?
Propping up my head now
Maybe my only escape
If only I could fix myself
With glue and masking tape

But that would be too easy
And life is no piece of cake
Still I have severe doubts
On how much more I can take

Switch Month

Appropriate me thinks
To change the style
Especially the month before
I tackle my next endeavor
Marriage will not be easy
But neither will carrying around
A silly dictionary
That randomly decides poetry topics
I could buy the game "Catch Phrase"
Or go through my Cranium cards
As a way to have quick words
But it seems unfair
This should be learning too
And I'm sure half these words
I will have never heard
Much less know the meaning of
Stationary is something
Life will never again be
Not that it ever really was
But the illusion is gone

Too much to ask

Today is Thursday
It is the final day of the month
The week up to now was horrid
And the month, not much better
So now I have to know
Is it too much to ask?
To have just one pleasant day
And I don't mean tomorrow
Yes, I will have paperwork tonight

And no, that is not exactly fun
But it is a procrastinated requirement
Therefore it has no bearing on the day
So far headed in the right direction
Woke up happy and rested
Played with my kittens and hugged my fiancée
Even got to use my computer, the obsession
If just this one day
I could be granted a complaint free
Cheerful experience with a few smiles
I could continue to push forward
If everything goes haywire
I need only remember Monday
Labor Day, a holiday, no work
September will be better

Transition

I am going to have to make a change
It won't be easy but maybe worthwhile
I have to start actively trying not to argue
When it is as natural to me as breathing
If only I could roll back time
Join the debate team and leave it there
But there are no such machines or methods
To do anything about the past
The new way is to change the subject
No matter what the foul, what the problem
Avoidance is my suggested path
Especially if I want life to stay great
I see no real choices here because I am
In fact very happy with the way things are
I don't need any more trouble than I am in
So I will do my best to try to change myself
The hardest change that is possible
But it starts today and must be taken that way
One day at a time, just like many problems
That I have faced in the past and overcome
As angry as I get I may need gallons of water
To cool my hot head when the moment arises

215

We all know it is one thing to say something
And quite another to actually follow through
Annoyed and absorbed by the world moving past
I have to make a priority out of one thing
And wait until I have accomplished it
Before I tackle anything else

Tragic Flaw

Story Book character often have a tragic flaw
My flaws, those tragic and worse, are abundant
One is when I get into a one sided discussion
That soon sounds like White Noise
Sometimes so loud that only I can hear
Another one raising my voice without control
This typically occurs after my terrible body language
And bad tone that leads one to believe I was an asshole
Even if I had a million dollars in my hand for you
Now we are at the top of a slippery iceberg
Which only gets worse when another alpha is introduced
Another man who thinks he knows the answers to everything
That is the makings of an atomic bomb
Hanging by a thin thread or the sound of a pin drop
And the simple answer I've had and ignored for years
Can make it all just go away
Change the subject, agree to disagree, and move on
Be a thinker and not a feeler
After all it does play into my self righteous hand
To be able to fix one more thing
Even if it's by simply changing the subject

Hell of a day to forget

What I feel I want right now is revenge
That stupid feeling that creeps up after anger
But it cannot be brought to fruition
For he is only a child
Yet referring to him in that manner
Only multiplies all of his anger

To a level none of us can control
Especially him, first and foremost
Yes to top it off I forgot my medicine
But who cares, it's not that important
The swearing and the threats
The harsh words and harsher looks
The slamming of doors and lockers
The fear his head will explode
Regardless of what I try to say
The tone and body language
They always give it away
Maybe I will never learn
And yes to top it off I forgot my medicine
But who cares, it's not that important
Or is it?

Samurai Cow

From my chair
Looking at a picture
Of a samurai cow
I wonder who thinks
Of these ideas
And why I paid
For this calendar
Of coupons I don't use
Glance right I see closed blinds
And realize I have no light
The fan is off and it is hot
Probably the computer running
This room closed off to the world
Only seen by four other humans
While I have lived here
Like the inside of a grave
Glance to the left I see animals
All sizes, colors, and shapes
Of a glorified stuffed animal collection
Barely missing any from being complete
And yet as complete as it will be
Wondering how better invested

And how much more happiness
The money could have brought
On my desk sit pictures
Of the one I love the most
Some from early childhood
And some from a few years back
None from now
She lives with me
I don't need pictures
Her image is ingrained in my head
From this place some call dull
Some call dusty and dirty
Some call boring and plain
With white empty walls
And a total lack of anything
Alive or natural
I feel most at home
And I write

Back at it

Tonight I'm going to church
It's actually less than three hours
The last time was this morning
But it wasn't for religious reasons
Just that pre-marital counseling
Tonight I am actually attending
At a different church
Who knows, maybe I'll sing
But will I be going along with it all
Or just laughing at the poor unfortunate souls
Who I think are wasting their time
Trying to change things or make a difference
With giving away money and praying
Really haven't decided yet
Just know I am going to go
Because I made a promise
To bring someone I know
And that is important, not breaking your word
Being trusted without a doubt

And occasionally getting a wake up call
I do hope it's one of those nights
Where I wander out the doors enlightened
But if it isn't I'll still be me
And you will still be you
Tomorrow will still be on the way
And I will have still written this

Word Fun

So anxious
Not able to hold it inside
Watching the clock
Speeding home
Having to know

Nothing
The answer wasn't there
It could be weeks

The next day the same
Every spare second
Spent checking
Like awaiting a letter in the mail
That was lost
And may never arrive

Time ticked away
Long
Longer

Then realizing he had it all along
Right under his nose
Never looking
In that spot
Where things tended
To not land

So anxious
Nothing

Time ticked away
In that spot

Electric Feelings

Now she's done it
Made my heart go a flutter
But I only know her first name

Why must everyone
Feel so insecure
About a technology
That seems so friendly

Yes; child pornography, stalkers, sickos, dirty old men
I guess I understand

But what are the true odds??
Why am I so analytical I must see things in numbers??
One in a thousand if that

But the lines have been drawn for a reason
And like rules and laws
I will abide or pay the price

And for the time being
I will smile
Because before, I had no name

Yesterday is so foreign
And my imagination so recent

Electric Feelings #2

My hearts a flutter
On the surface
It appears I'm in love
And I am, but with my wife and life
That statement, a flutter

Had nothing to do with it
Only an introduction to say
I'm excited
A rush and surge has filled me
Revived part of me I thought was dead
It's totally platonic, if even that
And most likely with my luck
Just more words without outcome
The subtle hints weren't clear enough
To make one see last time
The first name I know with no picture
No way of communicating with her
In a conversation
Was you

Sewn

Said too much
Another peep
A whisper
A breath
A thought

Now I must visit
The surgeon

Would you please
Stitch my lips
From one end to the other
So I won't have to worry

My thoughts
They keep escaping
Unavoidably

Take away my worry
Take away my guilt
Until someone has ESP

Then a lobotomy would be nice

Her Dreams

When she spoke
Of those dreams
She had the morning after
It was obvious
How much emotion
She left bottled up inside her soul

Dark and constant
Are the sharp pains he caused
Allowing the smallest problem
To get under his skin
And hollow him out

Sometimes only temporarily

Lashing in directions
Places normally unable to reach
And in return
The first words she spoke
Were the stern truth
Of her dream

Lack of sleep
Nightmares
Graphic descriptions
Pain

Was she really capable
Of such acts
He didn't think so
But he wasn't sure

Just another unconscious hint
To give her the respect she deserves

Still Magical

Tonight he would not fall again
Fall into the hole he had dug
He pressed his luck to a point
But then stopped and whispered
Those three words before falling asleep
Finally he listened to the advice
Being shouted from every direction
To never go to bed angry
Instead of escalating the situation further
And saying things he did not mean
The next day he felt no different
The soft expectation of another smile
Maybe a kiss or kind words
For finally stopping himself
Were not said to him
But in his heart he knew
He had done the right thing
And in the long run
Maybe years from now
This would make a difference

Decal

So proud of those stickers
Pressed on the bumper
And windows of his car
Shared statements and opinions

None original

Not his ideas
Just pre-made purchases
Aimed at laughs or anger

Just money wasted
On a semi-permanent declaration
Of free speech on a car
That would die within two years

But it made him feel more alive
To do what he pleased

Not with or against the norm
Just whimsical ideas
Like his clothes
Music and movie preferences
Thoughts and behaviors
Un-programmed and free

Sober

He slept, almost comatose
Until the phone rang
What time was it
Then came the pounding
Let me out
It screamed from inside
The liquor he carelessly swallowed
The night before
Thinking he had rid himself
Of that vile stuff
Having been so sick
He coughed up blood
Promises he started to make
Along with apologies
This won't happen again
But for how long
Months, maybe a year
Until he forgets
A few hours of fun
Are not worth a day of pain

A year

Sitting and Remembering
This time last year
When my pseudo-friend
Accused me falsely

My friend list dwindled
People walked by
Not even noticing me
Or choosing not to look
Months went by
And slowly I rediscovered
Who the real friends were
And which ones were made of cardboard
Appearing to make a crowd
But really just filling in
The huge gaps
In my ego

How unfair, like all of life
That one person
Can have so much pull
With just a lie

Combinations

The combination
Of sweat and heat
Lingering in this enclosed room
Promote ignoring my nose
And breathing from my mouth

The combination
Of vaulted ceilings
And loud voices echoing
Promote much more brain interpretation
Than actual hearing

The combination
Of her and I touching
Holding hands and kissing
Promote feelings of love
And disregard for the world

The combination
Of the descriptions above

And your interpretation
May promote the ideas of sex behind closed doors
When we sit at an indoor pool

It's too cold

It's too Cold
My fingers are numb
Brain frozen over
Needing another hot shower
But the hot water is out
For at least an hour
And I have twenty minutes
Until work begins
Painfully writing
Lines of Words without meaning
An inch at a time when I have none
In slow motion without a remote
The sun is no use
On days like today
When the wind whips and tears
My body astray
It's too cold

Under my Skin

What really gets under my skin
Talking about religion
Especially someone I just met
Asking too many questions
Why do so many
Consider it the most important thing
And if they do
That proves how nosy they are asking
At times I would appreciate
An a-religious marking
A tattoo, necklace, ring, hat
To signal, "Not Today!"
The pressure of responding

Is never as harmful
As their assumption
If I remain silent

Over and Over

Always trying
To fix the world
And not seeming
To move an inch
Even when the stakes are high
And the task is tiny
Attentions focused
In too many directions
Unable to multi-task
Failing over and over
Unable to remember
The simplest of rules
Accept the things
You cannot change
Which leaves only
Changing yourself

A small giggle

How I love you
Honestly, I don't know
You only burn me
And the fire never ends...
Either fire
My fire of feelings
And the fire engorging you
Burning your emotions as they emerge
Dousing you with love
Has no effect
And when I used the water bucket
Well, you got pissed
Embers and Ambers
Still red hot

Always reignite
What appeared only ash
Trying to escape
Is frivolous and wasteful
Our connection too deep
Both encompassed in one body

Quiet Game

Today a new game
But played for centuries
Who can hold their tongue
And be quiet the longest
Both determined to win
But his last words harsh
And I'm waiting for apology
So only silence remains
Big surprise
It took one whole hour
I am too competitive
And need a worthy opponent

Anticipation

Friday on the way
Four more days
And you blew the reward
Wonder if you'll move forward
Maybe if I neglect
To mention you weren't perfect
Or even close you'll be
Who I want to see
But once the truth is out
Pick you the alternate route
And put us all through hell
Until we ring the bell
Although disqualified
The rules you modified

One for One

Have it your way
Don't follow plan
Don't let me know
Whatever
Back and ready to resume the plan
But there is a catch
I didn't let you know...
I'm out!
The bartering has begun
The time one for one
Next time...well I'm the boss
Maybe one for ten
You will learn
To at least be polite
Not having manners
Determined by mood

Acquaintances

Doing nothing wrong
Expecting a good day
But he is obsessed
With his imaginary friends
You know the ones
Intimidated Acquaintances
Promising to call or walk
Without following through
In confusion he lashes out
All the usual threats
I say goodbye and walk away
But this is far from over
Now it's my turn
The phone rings
He listens to me
Without the chance to break me
So many empty promises made
But I feel better for now

Forcing apologies with consequences
Who really needs the help?

First Scream

Will I ever understand
This creature, woman
A complaint is made
But there is no answer
Sympathy and Empathy
Apathy and Action
I cannot fix it
And I tire of listening
Finally I act
The complaints have added
And with just one more
My head will explode
The cats are making noise
I grab the pet tote
And rush down the stairs
To enforce some time out
Then it begins
An ear piercing noise like never before, STOP!
Maybe I should lock her up for misbehaving
Waking the neighbors with her nonsense
But we can't talk
She is hiding in a closet
Shivering and afraid
To face me

Bliss

I was told we are different
What exactly?
Everything!
For how long?
Months!
Can I have an example?
NO!

Then how can I help?
That question's echo still ringing
There was no answer
Being me I released my frustrations quickly
Unplugging everything I could reach
Only to later put it back together
While taking out the trash
Vacuuming the house
And washing the dishes
We pretended it was fixed
Just like always

Limbo

Something happened
No feeling left
Detachment and Separation
Floating away
And then suddenly a tunnel
At one end darkness
At the other light
Looking like a snowy scene
Hating the cold
Moved towards the dark
No steps or footprints
Just motion to the other end
The end without a picture
But no matter how far
Glancing backwards
The snow side was still visible
After what seemed an eternity of movement
Still in the middle
Moved towards the light
But still stuck
Could this be hell
Thinking repeatedly
As seeing the light was possible
But forever frozen in place

Sweets

She asked if she could have a piece
And reached out and took one
Before he had a chance to answer
Slowly pushing it into her mouth
Those were the first words
That started a long lasting relationship
Between him and the woman of his nightmares
Who had become flesh before him
Her name was Candy
To most a stripper's name
But to him so appropriate and fitting
Because she started out so sweet
And like many candies
Having facets of all kinds
Only later became sour and without flavor
Leaving only distaste yet longing for more

Sailing

She looked in the mirror
And did not recognize
The stranger peering back
Into those deep green eyes
It was the same routine
Followed daily for years
Only today she looked past
Her makeup and hair
Deeper to a place invisible to most
The tears began to sail down her face
Not having felt anything in years
Unaware of the strain she was under
After a few minutes of crying
She vowed to take the time each day
So that when the day again came
To find herself she would already know

Taken Advantage

I've been warned
Thinking to myself
As she approaches
The nameless nurse
Since last we chatted
Many story fragments I've heard
From different trusted sources
That add to quite a tale
The basic theme simple
Keep my distance
Don't buy into the lies
Her love is only for money
Loving to go for a ride
As long as she doesn't pay
A greedy bitch like that
Can only get in my way
I hate to judge a stranger
But trust and value my friends
And when weighed against each other
The same group always wins

Forgotten

On the sidelines and forgotten
Although we visit the same places
Even still on the annual greeting card list
But you have no idea who I am
If the world shook hard enough
That a piece of the sky fell
And struck you like a marshmallow on the head
Would it jog your memory
Maybe it would take much more
Than a small cloud fragment
Although the damage of more mass
Could cause a total amnesia
Short of approaching with introduction
And explaining where our lifelines once crossed
It troubles me to even try
To help you remember me

Instincts

An older woman flirts with me
I think "can't you see the ring?"
And minutes later reprimanded like a child
Told only that she is trouble
As if I'm a cat following a shiny object
And must be punished for curiosity
But it's my friend, not my wife
There is a story behind this
Curiosity peaks and I begin to beg
Tell me this story, what do you know?
The lack of immediate answer
Shows me this is serious
Later communicated a basic idea
The woman is all out nuts
I figured she just liked to hit on young men
Where have all my instincts gone?

The Sign

Like a sign coming down
From God Almighty himself
He speaks those words I dread
"Today is gonna be a long day"
For someone not familiar
With the exact translation
Of what this means for him
It would be impossible to know
But I've heard it far too many times
Today will be terrible
Minutes will seem like hours
And the complaints will never end
Repeating the phrase I am tired
Or I have no freedom
Possibly followed up by discussing
How bad his life is, in his view
The only positive aspect

Which I can only consider okay
Is that I picked up on it early
And I can begin the eggshell walk

Names

There may be a day
When I forget your name
And if I never learned it
You may be lost forever
So I force myself threatening dire consequences
To write, to speak, to photograph
Leaving a path of post-its
To remind me who you are
I'm not the only one
Slowing being absorbed by the nothing
But unable to say no
I join the pool of ashes
Being blown by winds of change
So I have no eyes to look into
And no voice to cry out
For the help I need
Maybe someone will change the world
But I've long given up the hope
That as I drown in pain
Someone will understand me

Wind Up

Either I'm psychic
Or the world beneath me
And all that surround it
Are becoming mechanical
As I know time will pass
That the second hand will tick
So it seems I can predict
Exactly how the day will go
My laughter becomes more rare
Because it takes a true human

Not another wind up doll
To say something original
Longing for the day
When a wrench will be thrown
Into the spokes of repetition
That has become our life
A routine without variables
A one way street
Without intersections
In a desert

My Turn

Sometimes I wish
God would give me a turn
To help me understand myself
And her more completely
Knowing just how selfish and greedy
Of pure of heart I am
And the impossibility of a job
That involves the whole world
How many more ears I would need
To differentiate all the voices and prayers
Decided which were justified
And give even a simple yes or no nod
Putting life into a perspective
I could not possibly get on my own
Seeing through someone's eyes
Much greater than my own

Starting Over

The time has arrived
When the bitter cold
Brings out the words
That haunt my soul
Perhaps Autumn is so wonderful
After the brilliant colors fade
And the first frost kills everything

Allowing the release to begin
SO much time passed
From pen reaching paper
It's no longer natural
And I must overwork
But a beginning and end
Everything must have
And this years beginning
Is now

Before the Wedding

For weeks now I've been asked daily
"So...are you nervous yet?"
I respond honestly "No, not yet."
But I'm beginning to realize it's "not ever"
It seems to me the wedding is easy
Why worry about the formal announcement
We are already married in most senses
I don't need a certificate or ceremony to tell me
We live, eat, sleep, talk, drive, play, and rest together
More than many married couples I know
I think we are both more nervous
About hours over ocean in an airplane
Did this common question about our composure
Develop in the long ago past and continue as tradition
Or do some people really not understand what it means
Until they reach the altar and begin to crack
I need only know a few things:
I am in love with Anne and she with me
We've agreed to talk and work out problems
And forever together still seems too short

Frustrated

On a day like today
Three months ago
I would have bought something
And spent more money than I could

But that must be the difference
Now I don't really have any desires
It's not that spending would not help
But that I have nothing to buy
Almost as if the part of my brain
That differentiates between wants and needs
Just flushed the wants down a toilet
And left me with needs that are already fulfilled
The question remains
How do I release my frustration
Thinking weekly chess nights against experts
Will be like fighting a black belt
No matter how hard I try
I will not win
But I can learn a lot
Without hurting myself or others

Poor Baby

Everything should be the way he says
Me! Me! Me! I! I! I!
The world owes me
Then like a scratch in the record
He begins again
Very good selective memory
Insisting on full attention by the room
When repeating himself for the millionth time
Disagree even one time and you're an enemy
Plotting against him forever

Space

Why are you so close to me
I need some space
Before I saw your face
I figured you were a minion
Someone sent here by the pastor
To make sure I didn't try anything
Like disrupting the service

Even I wouldn't disrupt church
But I turned towards you
Younger than me
Apparently just enjoying the back row
Where the projected song words are illegible
Still so close, I smiled when you left
And stretched out while refusing communion
I think I need to find something new
Without bibles and crosses

At the place again

Guess where I'm stuck again
Letting one know I'm terribly uncomfortable
Isn't really the hint you need
To realize it is Sunday night
That's right, I'm at the Baptist Church
I feel like a vampire watching sunrise
Burning and blinding me to even look up
So I don't
I refuse to even open my mouth
My nose can breathe in this pollution
But my beliefs vary so much from these
I would prefer an hour of stinky public restrooms
At least then I could giggle
At the various messages and phone numbers
Written inside the stalls and walls
This stench is far worse

Music Preference

Thrashing guitars stacked up
Playing fast loud melodies
Not exactly relaxing to most
More likely to energize
But they reach him on another level
Past the lyrics and beats
The musicians seem to understand
How he feels deep inside

It has so much power
Clearly it seems alive
Just not the way expected
Perhaps it's a reminder
He is stuck in a circle
And no matter the path
It seems the hard way
So he runs in place
Like a treadmill or a track
Exercising, Living, but not traveling
From point A and back
Almost like a dream

Put yourself First

I want to come first
She sang along with the radio
Speaking of how she should be seen
From a male
And she still didn't understand
Lesson numero uno in life
That putting yourself first
Is the only way to succeed
After one has reached the top
And decided for sure that
They love themselves completely
Only then can they put others first
Most of us are constantly
At battle internally with ourselves
Trying to accept one thing at a time
Instead of everything forever

Retentivity

I have retentivity over my tears
Although I wish it was not so
I can retain them for what seems an eternity
And never once so much as blink

But I do not want this curse
And slowly but surely I am making steps
Towards losing my ability to hold things inside
And just let my emotions be moving like rivers
It is unhealthy to feel something
But for it to not show on the outside
Never able to show other people how you feel
Because that same stupid face is always forward
No matter how bad I feel inside
My body language, tone of voice
The ability to portray my true feelings
Is locked inside some unlockable safe
Although my feelings are not retained inside me
I can feel them ten times over for the lack
Of ability to let one ounce of feeling out
With the exception of a laugh or smile

Fixated

Some people are just fixated
That they are something they are not
Like those who believe they are vampires
And actually drink blood to prove it
Having expensive tooth alterations
Wearing all black far past being goth
Watching movies and reading books
To find a character to imitate correctly
Such a pathological attraction
Is unhealthy for humans to have
Over a person, an idea, or a thing
All lead in the same direction
To the asylum
Where you can rant all day
With padded walls and a jacket
That makes your arms useless

Ganging Up

He feels the pressure
Never feeling he is correct
The family and friends
Gather together to fix him
Lashing out he yells
"You always gang up on me"
The situation rarely matters
Just that it's not his idea
His friends and family
Pray for the way
To make him think it's his idea
To help him brainstorm
He stands like a pyramid
Stuck in the sand and unmovable
Not easily overcome by brainwashing
Unless it is by another pyramid
He tries a million times over
To be the people person he wants to be
But unable to take a step in any direction
He is left rooted in limbo

Glory of God

At church he kept hearing
For the glory of God
That's where all the focus should be
But it did not all add up
Always he had been taught
First love yourself in order
To allow yourself to love others
And assumed that meant God too
What good is an empty vessel
Putting God first
He is like a mannequin
No one knows what he thinks
Whereas taking the time
To love yourself first
Gives you the power
To actually make a difference
Disagreeing with the specific church

He continued his mission
To find a place where he belonged
And could follow his own heart

Miscalculated

He was like a broken machine
Unable to add things up
Not the mathematical errors
The errors in judgment about others
He miscalculated people
Expected too little or too much
Thinking everything could fit into a formula
Was the actual miscalculation
Fighting back against the world
With practicums, theorems, diagrams
But nothing that could even explain himself
Just a lost person falling out of reality
Because the grip he had was so fragile
That the slightest blow of the wind
Turned the world upside down
And he started over again

Querulous

She was that type of woman
One that could never find the good
One that despite all the beauty
Saw the shambles and dregs of the world
She was querulous
Plenty of things to say
Many opinions to share
But not even one positive thing
When the mood struck her
She could talk for hours on end
About how things could be better
And how the world was ripping her off
It was almost fact
An inevitable truth

That she would always be alone
Never learning how to love or be loved

The mold

Ever so often one comes along
That breaks the mold
Not falling into the usual description
Of who she fell in love with
Brains and dialogue always
Turned out to be important in the end
And he had these qualities
But usually she fell for the muscle
The athletic type without much fat
It almost assured they took care of themselves
And were not heavy drinkers or addicts
Which is most definitely a plus
This guy just made her laugh
Made her feel young again
Of course it helped that he wasn't wild
But the first thing she noticed was his smile
Unable to act upon her hidden impulses
Because both were already in relationships
One relationship new and one very serious
She subdued her feelings and never let him know
If only she had known
He shared the same feelings
And it could have formed a friendship
That would never be broken

Dr Visit

Last name
First name
Birth date
Address
Phone Number

Now I have a number

No longer a person
Just another notch
Another co-pay
Another puzzle

Start the timer
How fast can we finish
Most patients in the day
Wins a prize
A free coffee

All the different symptoms
Cross contaminate
One another
While waiting
To be called back

The other pole

This season
For some reason
This year it means
So much less
The medication perhaps
Has its mishaps
But I feel jealous
Of a simple holiday
Last year and before
I always had more
To give out to friends
Or just did not care
But now with the bills
I've cut down on frills
And my gift of happiness
Well everyone already has it
I'm all in a panic
Being on so manic
So instead of the happy
All get the angry
My temper so hot

Making all in sight rot
When it all ends
Then again I'll have friends
People who care
With whom I can share
The better side
That had to hide
For this year when Christmas came
It was all I had to blame
By taking all my smiles
Road blocking them for miles

Botched Christmas 06'

The plan has been set into motion
Five to gather together
For a family experience at last
But of the three
Original members
One backs out
Along with her guest
Leaving only three
Gathering for a holiday
But not as special
As the plan had been
Seemingly never
Does the plan come to fruition
With this person
Let downs
One after another
Leaving everyone thinking
When will they give up
Trying to save a space
For someone
Who doesn't want it
A waste of time
A memory
A part of the family
Who wants out

Your game

I don't enjoy this game
Taking away the natural element
Trying to be
What I am not
Acting another way
Thinking another way
Writing another way
Talking another way
It's nonsense
I have and always
Will be me
Some things about myself
Not even I can change
SO I say
Take it or leave it
I will not play this game
I might love you
But I do love me
As I am
Forever

Clubs

In-audible to others
This bothersome ringing in my ears
Has an almost sleepless story behind it
Surrounded in a pale cloud
Of strong tobacco smoke
Microphone amplified screaming
And deafening instrumentals
Of guitar, bass, drums, and samples
Last night I stood in one place
Close to five hours
For one last hoorah
Of a band I adore
Some lyrics I had never understood
Became clear at that time

But the ringing
Does not allow my brain to recall
I've finally reached the first milestone
That is not enjoyable
About growing up
I can no longer do this
Much too used to seats
Inside large auditoriums or coliseums
For a shoulder to shoulder packed hours
In a rinky dink club
One activity I've done for ten years
Has now reluctantly been knocked off my list
To avoid the pain
Of the ringing

A kiss

Once one is older
Not too more
Than she is now
A realization becomes clear
Best friends for life
Is usually just a phrase
Being much more rare than "true love"
Best friends don't stop over a small mistake
Like a kiss, even an inappropriate kiss
Causing by a confusion of feelings
Does not mean the end to a friend
Whereas love
In its many facets
Can end quite abruptly
Over so many factors outside control
Of any of the ones involved
Often the friendship it creates
Contains more love
Than it began with
And only makes life more full
Of those surprises
We live for

Themes from Stories

When he chopped down the cherry tree
They asked him three times and more
And all the crows did not change his mind
He decided it and eventually blamed another
Being so honest up to this point
Even perhaps always since this point
They punished the other without remorse
The suffering was to be an example
Why stepping forward was so important
Nothing changed
Just a them in a story
Parents tell children
When no one is truly honest
The world cannot be split in two
Good and bad
But is grey, dependant on opinion
And thus, will always be

Fatalist

I am too comfortable
To take the worries of the world
And place them on my shoulders
Rather, I will ignore them with a fatalist attitude
No matter what I do
Things will end up the same
Feudalism clearly states
This is my lot
To live and die with it
My participation matters not
So I stopped reading
I stopped watching the news
Simply decided the pain of the world
Was the world's alone
And my hands needed not to be washed
Because they were already clean

Goliath

There you are
The two of you
David and Goliath
Not really enemies
More like friends
But not exactly
Just people side by side
Trying to be civilized
One of you, usually solving problems with anger and force
Getting their way by default
But today the tables have turned
Young David forgot the sling
But he holds the Kryptonite
And he will not be denied
With a powerful comeback
To every negative comment
David insists on a realism and positivity
And Goliath reluctantly understands
He must crumble under the pressure
If the original plan is to be carried out
This time without a choice
Goliath is forced to relax
With the hope that someday
He will learn it on his own

Bent and Broken

With smiles and lollipops
Laughter and listening
He kept going the extra mile
Bending just a little further
Each time it seemed
The outburst of the century was near
His patience grew ever so
Allowing it to blow over
Confused about what was important
He seemed to bend for the wrong reasons

And stay stern for the wrong as well
The ones he loved got a raw deal
Then the day came they had predicted
The last gram of straw he could hold
Was loaded on a back fully bent
To the point of breaking
But they didn't add a single gram
Or several or even an ounce
The next thing thrown upon him
Was ten pounds worth of material
Purposely meant to break him
Expanding and contracting
Pushing and pulling
Praying for a way to balance
But he crumbled for a split second
Before the beast inside him came alive
Ripping through the tons of weight above him
Like it was nothing
To get free of all his burdens
But instead of destroying and decimating
He simply assumed the stance
He had before the pile began
And started over
Remembering this time
Loved ones come first

Human

When I awake
I realize that it's the longest
In the last twenty four hours
We have gotten along
Without an argument
And it will continue to grow
Until we speak
So I choose to be silent
This is not the life I wanted
But the only one keeping it this way
Is me
Even with the force of ten armies

Using torture chambers
Would have no effect
I refuse to back down
I refuse to let it go
I refuse to drop it
I refuse to be human

Mistakes

Too many times already
I've asked you to go away
To leave me alone
To stop talking to me
And the worst phrase of all
That I don't care
What you think
What you feel
What you know
Seeming to anyone including you
That I don't need you
And I don't want you
My lack of ability
To verbally express myself
Orally and not in written word
Has cursed my entire life
Up to this point
But I am ready for a change
I just ask for your help
Point out all my stupid mistakes
So I can at least try
To be who you see
When you look
Into my eyes

Interpretations

The way he interpreted what I said
Made me crack a sarcastic smile
But I did not tell him what I meant

I just left the conversation there
Without an ending
But without an insult
To his intelligence

These misunderstandings
Are becoming ever so more common
As he thinks he knows me better
And feels more comfortable
Contributing to my flow
Of nonsensical thoughts
Just rambling

Not yet has a peep of my laughter
Escaped into a rumbling roar
Showing how silly the comment was
Not yet have I let him know
He has no clue
And never has
As to what I speak of

Usually talking just to hear myself
Instead of a subject that I hate to discuss
Although interrupted many times
Still better to hear the repetition
In my own head
Than the imaginary
That is ever changing

According to his mood
On that day

My Bubble

I have to escape this world of the past
My past
These haunting thoughts that keep me awake
No one else
I can't change even my own perception
Of the memory of anything up to this point

But I try
Over and over again
This bubble I live inside
Just grows
A day at a time
To insure that I don't think of the present
Not just my present
But anyone's
And I don't have a pin
Or knife
Anything sharp enough to break free
Letting go of this past time
And grasping the here and now
I would trade a year of the old
For a day of the new

Anger Haiku Story

One day after time
To turn over the anger
That I want to share

Furious Silence
Fills the room between us two
No breathing at all

Insecurities
Could be cut through with a tear
Instead a scream

Both to separate
Into worlds of their own build
To cool from boiling

Attempts to amend
This explosion of nothing
Shunned with quick outbursts

Until all remains

Are two who love too deeply
To just let it go

8th Grade

Dreaming about the beginning
Back when I had to write for school
Required to come up with a simple rhyme
With a deep meaning
Armed with only Shel and Shakespeare
I began the poem with four words a line
Hoping that at the end
Some awesome Godly intervention
Would give me the ending
That I was looking for all along
I thought I had failed
But the teacher saw it another way
Beckoning me to enter a contest
And giving me a perfect grade
I followed his instruction again
And the contest was won
Only later did I learn
After my heart had begun to pour out
All the feelings I had onto paper
That the contest was another one of those…
Everyone wins and they hope you buy the book
I had won nothing, published but worthless
The book was a sham
Over ten years, many dreams and poems later
I still write
And soon will have a book
But it's for myself
Not to get rich
Not to prove something
Not to feel superior
Just because
The spark he ignited in me never died
And where ever he is
Maybe someday he'll see my name
And smile with me

Without him I would lack the courage
To be me

Deep End

Sitting at the bottom
Of this pool
Clearing out all thoughts
While I breathe out all air
Pushing to a limit
Twelve feet below the surface
Of definite survival
And possible death
The most important things
Flood my mind
As my ears pop
Under the pressure
Too exhausted
For playing possum games
With the on duty lifeguard
I come up inhaling
That sweet gas of life

In touch

Finally I broke a barrier
The wall between emails and phone calls
To an in person visit
Meeting the children of two people
I last saw when they were children themselves
Equal with me then

But I am still a child
I am no parent
I am no role-model
I have no house
I only pretend
That all those lessons I was taught

From then to now
Were learned

Of

It wont be long now
Until the thoughts of desperation
Overcome me
And won't let me be
Of what I could have done
Of what I could have been
Of the mistakes I've made
Of the games I've played
Looking up to the clouds
And down to the ground
Unable to see heaven or hell
I just crawl back into my shell
Waiting for impending disaster
Thinking of how I would be judged
But it hasn't happened so far
I still have time to wish upon a star
Arise from this funk of a life
That began innocent and changed
To a terrible monstrosity
Where I could never be free
Ask for forgiveness just one more time
And actually mean it in my soul
Not for just up to this point
But for forever more

Backtalk

The other day
His chance finally arrived
Shining like a diamond in the rough
He could respond to the statements
That never make a bit of sense
Without fear of punishment or consequences
His ace in the hole

257

Guaranteed his safety
And he jumped at it
Giving someone a piece of his mind
And afterwards the someone said only one thing
"I'm sorry"
It may never happen again
But it felt like a revolution
And he's still smiling

One side

Every week
The same stories
Nothing ever accomplished
New words
A foreign concept
But I only hear one side
Seeming so honest
Yet very secretive
Version after version
Every week
The same stories
But I only hear one side
I long to put the pieces together
To the half finished
Jigsaw chunk of life
Yet every week
The same stories
And I only hear one side

Is this real

So hard to decide
Is this real
Could I actually
Be getting back all these friends
Or is it the gullibility of myself
That I haven't looked in the eye for three years
Part of me being held back

This is too good to be true
I begin to ask the usual questions
Do they want something?
Yes, but it's practically free
Except maybe an hour of my time
No money, gifts, drugs, hurt feelings
The important questions can't be answered
Until this ends
How long will it last?
A week, a month, a year
The decision is already made
But in a week or two
I will know if it was the right one
Or if I fell for it again
And got used

Waiting for Humbugs

One more week
Until the holiday hits
I feel like I'm not prepared
Maybe no one is
But I know this will be different
Some of the gifts have not arrived
And in a week
The chances are they wont
I would love to take a short vacation
Or maybe a long one
Until all this seasonal mess has ended
Until people have forgotten Christmas
And who got a present from whom
The game of present tag bores me
I almost wish the Grinch would swoop down
Take all the trees and presents away
And leave us like Who-ville
Except we all know
We are human, not Whos
We would not join together and sing
We could not think it is okay

Everything would be ruined
And like the average day

<u>In search of</u>

Struggling for a way
To find one element
He has lost
That makes him human

Tears

He starts with sad music
Quickly moving to depressing film
Artwork, poetry, novels
Nothing is working

Maybe his own pain...
Cutting himself with a dull blade deeply
It aches but his eyes like dry stone ignore it

Maybe the pain of others
Visiting someone close to him
He spits out ugly lies
And says all his goodbyes
Watching them sniffle and suffer
Still nothing

Maybe it's in his brain
Head butting the concrete wall
In an attempt to rearrange
Coming to the conclusion
He cannot cry
Gouges out an eye
To feel liquid flow down his face once more
Before he dies

<u>Distorted</u>

She made a promise
Thinking of one so pure
In his eyes
He drew expectations
That were distorted
And not followed
The promise was not meant
To be forever
But for the time being
Her gentleness confused him
And all the season of his life
He stayed confused

Overrated

He's been waiting months
For this day

Alone

No plans

Nothing overhanging
But now that it's here
Reality sets in

Just like a child
With a jealousy complex
He only wanted what he could not have
Only an hour after awaking

The simple truth
Just another day

Alone

What are accidents?

Define accident in your head
Now I ask you
Whose bright idea was "accident prevention"
I'd like to give him or her an award
For swindling the world
Out of more money
Than I could count in a week
It's an oxymoron
First one can't really pre-vent
If you do then you've changed the variables
Would it have happened that way
One thing is for sure
You will never know
Then we add accident
Happening but not purposefully
You cannot prevent a mistake
First one would have to make the mistake on purpose
Then there is no mistake, just action
Following is the prevention of action
Simply put, reaction
So by rearranging some common knowledge
Actions have reactions
Someone made a bundle
Why didn't I think of that

Buddingbrook Lane

Back as a child
Living on Buddingbrook Lane
Where at one end
Then sign spelled it Buddin
And the other Budding
But the brook was the important part
Because we had one
Now and for years
The running water
Which ran only through a few yards
And ended pouring into a lake

In my front yard
Has vanished
Along with the fish and life all around it
Thinking back it was likely
Rain and Sewer drainage
From the yet to be annexed suburb
Of a growing city we thought was safe
Far from it then and now further
But it will always hold the memories
Of friends and growing up
Fishing for hours with nothing to catch
Besides old tires and beer cans

Elm Street

I used to think of it
Only as the name of a tree
Like all other roads
It had to have a name
Until one day watching a movie
One of the first roles of Johnny Depp
I watched a woman get torn apart
By something invisible to everyone else
This was the boogie man
He had all the signs a child needed
And the burnt face and claws later revealed
Only closed the deal
Such began my utter fascination with horror
And my desensitization to life
Soon I was using sharp sticks
To pick up the road kill with my friends
And bury it in a pet cemetery
Waiting for results
That never came
While much of what was real in me
Was flushed down a drain

Names Don't Match

As I came to understand in school
Names like Martin Luther King
What they stood for
And how almost every city in the US
Had a street named after him
The bitter irony began
Growing worse as soon as I could drive
These were the ghettos
Where I'm from
If you are white, you don't go there
Especially at night, alone
Similar to Church street
There may be or have been
A church at one time
But that doesn't take away
The prostitutes and the homeless
That our country has created
Wandering the usual places
Looking for a break
They will never find
Until the fairy Godmothers
Decide to help out more than just Cinderella

Always Denied

All those years
Of religion
Forced into my head
And I can't remember
Which disciple denied Christ
Three times before the cock crowed
But I remember last week
The opinions of a crowd
One after another
Asking
"Is this her?"
No, two voices giggled back in unison
Yes the age range was right
But the interpretation
Of two friends

Enjoying a good conversation
On a cold evening
As flirting?
Well, maybe it is
Maybe it isn't
But she is not my wife

Friend

"How long will you be my friend"
Not exactly what he said
But close enough
And I responded something like:
As long as you need me to be
I know there are days
You'd rather be free
To really not have to put up with me
But usually the pros
Far outweigh the cons
And when I leave
So do all things that came with me
All those things we listed
The list was long and exhaustive.
"Don't you get a choice or is it up to me?"
Again maybe not exact words
But close enough
And to that I simply smiled
And replied
"No
The choice is all yours"
I felt his uneasiness
As we changed the subject
Until the next day

An arrogant saying

Hearing this recently
The need again developed
To state and explain

What he felt
Was the most ignorant saying in the world
Just these five words
"I know how you feel"
To simplify why
This is so excessively ignorant
An example
Someone close has died
Another trying to console approaches
And makes the statement
Bla Bla... I know how you must feel... bla bla bla
Nothing
And I do mean NOTHING!
Could be further from the truth
But programmed by the ignorant
We speak without analyzing
What this means
One can never
FEEL as you do
They are not you!

The world is full of imbeciles

Sacrifice

Now that my understanding
Is beginning to increase
I wish life
Was more like a game of chess
Able to plot out
Several moves ahead
Knowing an answer
To whatever situation appeared
Understanding sometimes
A sacrifice
Is inevitable
To win the game
Unfortunately
Two problems arise
Life is not a game

You cannot win
And secondly
No matter the number
Of possibilities in chess
Life has so many more
One is unable to calculate
Anything but a formula
That creates random numbers

Butting in

He was talking to someone
Another approached
Introductions made
Then he simply listened
Not really butting in
As much as hovering
Spying on the conversation
And when they decided to depart
He followed as if he was part
Of the group
Why oh why
Must he always do this
In trying to be part
He sticks out
In a BAD way
And I get asked
"Do you know him?"
"Can't you explain this?"

But I can't

A Christmas poem

Seeing something
I did not expect
Especially on a Monday
I cringed
A man in my room

My bedroom nonetheless
Placing presents on the floor
Which was the only place
To get under
The one foot tall
Fake Christmas tree
We had on the dresser
The suit and beard
The colors
His round size
Could it really be him
Of course
I awoke from the dream
But the presents remained
My wife wanted to surprise me
On our first Christmas together
What a sweet idea
I gave her a hug while she slept
And fell back into a slumber

<u>Even Now</u>

Even now married
When I think about the women who have hurt me
No matter how long ago in the past
The feelings still linger and last
It could be the solution to the questions

Why can't I show my emotions
Why will I never cry

The barracks and vices I have been through
To jump over flaming hoops
And run naked over frozen mountains
Just to get their approval
Left me nothing of what I once was
But it could be the solution to the questions

Why can't I show my emotions
Why will I never cry

I once had such a good ear to listen
To the problems each of them shared
Wanting to be a knight in shining armor
Wishing I could help them
Now I know that was always impossible
They just used me to move forward
Leaving me pushed face down in the mud
But it left me with the solution to these questions

Why can't I show my emotions
Why will I never cry

.

About the Author

Chris Sapp was born and raised in W-S, NC.
He has been writing poetry for most of his life.
The words, he writes for a personal release, and not for the purpose of making money, but to share some of his feelings with the world.
"If only one person who reads this decides they have the inspiration to write down what they feel, then I have accomplished my goal."

Chris graduated from UNC Asheville with a Bachelors of Arts in Psychology and works with special populations, making a difference one day at a time. He also enjoys working online and playing video games. He loves amusement parks and his family, especially his beautiful new wife Anne.

Other books by Chris Sapp include:

Emotional Fragments Book 1
Emotional Fragments Book 2
Emotional Fragments Book 3
Emotional Fragments Book 4
Ten Years on Paper Book 1
Ten Years on Paper Book 2

All available at LuLu.com

http://www.lulu.com/clockworkchris

272